Southern
NATIONAL FORESTS

Southern
NATIONAL FORESTS

Sharyn Kane and Richard Keeton

National Forests of America

ABOUT THE AUTHORS

Sharyn Kane and Richard Keeton are a married team of writers based in Marietta, Georgia. *National Forests of the South* is their third book and also contains a number of their photographs. Avid outdoor enthusiasts, they have traveled extensively throughout the United States, with special emphasis on the Southern region described in the following pages. Their other two books, both published by the National Park Service, are factual accounts of natural and human history spanning many centuries.

They are also frequent magazine contributors on a wide range of topics, from environmental issues to high technology, and as accredited artists with the National Endowment for the Arts present writing workshops and give readings from their work.

ACKNOWLEDGMENTS

There are millions of acres in the Southern National Forest System, and we were fortunate to see many of them, often guided by Forest Service employees. Without fail, they were dedicated and eager to showcase the magnificent lands in their care. We are especially grateful for their willingness to extend their work days well past quitting time to share just one more hiking trail or one last fishing hole, whatever the weather. Public affairs specialists in particular were invaluable resources, but many others were also helpful, and while space prohibits naming them all, we remember each one with warm appreciation.

Thanks, too, to Dick Hoffmann and Mary Jo Hess with the Forest Service Regional Office in Atlanta for their many efforts on behalf of this book. And one final nod to John Grassy, our editor at Falcon Press, for his sound judgment, careful pen, and infectious wit.

NATIONAL FORESTS OF AMERICA SERIES

Copyright © 1993 by Falcon Press Publishing Co., Inc., Helena and Billings, Montana

Published in cooperation with the Forest Service, U.S. Department of Agriculture

Design, typesetting and other prepress work by Falcon Press, Helena, Montana. Printed in Korea.

Library of Congress Cataloging-in-Publication Data

Kane, Sharyn, 1950-
      Southern national forests / written by Sharyn Kane and Richard Keeton.
            p.   cm. -- (National forests of America)
      ISBN 1-56044-131-3
      1. Forest reserves--Southern States--Guidebooks.
2. National parks and reserves--Southern States--Guidebooks.
I. Keeton, Richard, 1946-   .   II. Title.   III. Series.
SD426.K36 1993
917.504--dc20   93-9514
                                                        CIP

Front cover photo:
Nantahala National Forest, North Carolina. BILL LEA

Title page photo:
Big Creek, North Carolina. LARRY ULRICH

Back cover photos:
Mountain trout fishing. BILL LEA
Sky Bridge, Daniel Boone National Forest, Kentucky. ADAM JONES
Golden Ragwort, Virginia. STEVE SOLUM

Contents

SOUTHERN NATIONAL FORESTS

Whitaker Point is a prime vantage spot for enjoying the Upper Buffalo Wilderness in the Ozark National Forest. The headwaters of the Buffalo National River begin in the wilderness, a rugged stretch of deep valleys and forested hills. Beyond the wilderness, the river continues northeast. ABERNATHY & ROBERTS

Introduction

Nurturing a national treasure

Standing atop one of the high peaks in the Appalachian Mountains, the view takes in deep green woodlands unfolding towards the horizon in every direction. Farther south, the cool, clear waters of a pristine spring flow between lush palms and palmettos, and tropical birds wade near the shore. To the west, pastel blossoms of thousands of wildflowers nod and bend in wide grass prairies.

These and other portraits of the national forests of the South could fill a thousand galleries, with something to appeal to every taste. There are more than twelve million acres in thirty-four forests in fourteen states and Puerto Rico in the region, and their visual splendors and opportunities for recreation are as rich and varied as their vital natural resources.

Modern-day explorers chart their way with compasses through rugged canyons where prehistoric people once traveled, while other adventurers navigate the thrilling rapids of a white-water river. Near dusk, a character costumed for the late 1800s tells tall tales around the campfire about bears and mountain lions, while a trail guide explains the many uses of plants and trees.

Ghosts of the past seem to beckon to have their stories heard as well, of how they once climbed these same peaks and fished in these waters. Many of their names are inscribed in history books: Davy Crockett,

Daniel Boone, Stonewall Jackson. But most others are long forgotten. Only remnants of their homes and businesses remain and most of these are being reclaimed by nature. Hikers travel the old Indian trails and wagon roads without knowing what important links these passages once were.

Trucks loaded with timber travel over newer roads, headed to sawmills where the felled trees will be shaped into wood products for use worldwide. Nearby, wells steadily pump oil and gas through pipelines, and these resources, too, will be refined for consumers.

As years pass, fewer people are left who remember how the lands once looked that now comprise the national forests of the South. In place of the millions of acres of healthy trees growing today, there once was

widespread devastation. Only tree stumps remained as far as the eye could see, as one great forest after another was indiscriminately logged with little thought of the consequences. Farmlands were equally despoiled. Unwise planting and harvesting practices had allowed crucial topsoil to erode and gaping gullies to form. Erosion was equally rampant where the original forests once stood. Without trees to hold soils in place, the ground washed away in great rivers of mud. Flooding increased, compounding the ruin, and the heavy silt in rivers and streams harmed water supplies and killed fish. Other wildlife also suffered as their habitats were destroyed. Uncontrolled hunting nearly eliminated white-tailed deer, black bear, and turkey in regions where they once numbered in the thousands.

Conservationists, particularly President Theodore Roosevelt and Gifford Pinchot, the first American trained as a forester, became alarmed and moved into action. Roosevelt and Pinchot worked to put many of the neglected landscapes under the protective umbrella of the United States government. And Pinchot, first chief of the Forest Service, steadily built

Left: Preserving historic sites, such as the Stewart Cabin in North Carolina's Nantahala National Forest, and educating the public about their significance, are among tasks performed by the USDA Forest Service. LAURENCE PARENT

Above right: Fraser firs are sensitive to environmental conditions and are one of many diverse species in the forests. STEVEN Q. CROY

Below right: Flame azaleas blanket forest mountainsides, while other wildflowers decorate fields and stream banks. ADAM JONES

the agency to restore and manage the lands for the benefit of the public.

After careful stewardship by the Forest Service, an agency of the United States Department of Agriculture, (USDA), the scars have largely healed. Over the years, entire forests were replanted, many by the Civilian Conservation Corps. The "CCC" was a federal government program that provided jobs to young unemployed men during the economic depression of the 1930s. Housed and fed in military-style conditions near work sites, the young men also built many of the roads in the forests, as well as dams to protect watersheds, and cabins and other shelters for recreation.

Fulfilling the vision of the foresighted conservationists of the early 1900s, the forests and two Texas grasslands continue to be managed under the concept of multiple use. This approach protects soils, water, and wildlife habitat while enhancing outdoor recreation and providing business with access to timber, minerals, and other consumable resources. Twenty-five percent of the receipts reaped by the federal government from these commercial uses are returned to the counties where the forests are located. No commercial activities, however, take place in the designated wilderness areas. Indeed, not even machinery is permitted in these regions, where it is possible to

gain a sense of what the undiscovered land was like long ago.

This tapping of resources distinguishes national forests from national parks, where recreation is the principal activity. Hunting is another distinction between them. While prohibited in national parks, hunting is allowed in national forests in cooperation with state game and fish agencies. Hundreds of acres are set aside in many forests for special wildlife management areas where logging and other activities foster improved hunting, and where thousands of ponds, streams, and lakes are improved and stocked for fishing.

Nongame animals are also receiving increasing special attention from the Forest Service. Many of the forests provide some of the last refuge for endangered and threatened species of animals and plants. Protecting habitats is a task of ever-growing dimensions, and one often fraught with controversy as areas are restricted from timber harvesting and other uses to preserve them for various species. Wildlife biologists and botanists have joined ranks with traditional foresters among the 4,000 employees in the Southern Region as the agency seeks to serve disparate needs.

Representatives from many other professions also serve important roles, many of them behind the scenes. Real estate experts continue to acquire land for the forests, often arranging mutually beneficial property exchanges with landowners. Archeologists survey thousands of acres every year, pinpointing sites with cultural significance, and, when possible, furthering knowledge about past human life. Geologists, engineers, firefighters, law enforcement officers, and computer, budget, recreation, and public information specialists are among a few of the others important to the successful management of the forests.

Private individuals and organizations are also significant in enhancing these national treasures. Volunteers perform tasks impossible to complete were it not for outside assistance, from maintaining hiking trails to building footbridges. Clubs, schools, and businesses contribute funds to improve wildlife habitat, conduct

research, and rehabilitate old facilities. The list of what more can be done continues to grow.

Millions of people visit the national forests of the South every year. Some drive scenic byways, routes designated for their particularly pleasing views. Others stop for picnics in shady settings. Some campers enjoy pitching their tents for free almost anywhere they choose, while others prefer developed campgrounds suitable for recreational vehicles. Hikers, horseback riders, cyclists, cross-country skiers, and

From the wetlands of Texas to the estuaries of the Atlantic Coast, water found within the national forests of the South is crucial to the well-being of human, plant, and animal life.
ROBERT W. PARVIN

off-road vehicle enthusiasts travel the thousands of miles of trails coursing through the forests. Rock climbers, scuba divers, swimmers, sailors, and water skiers also find ideal spots to pursue their passions. Wildlife watchers and photographers will find few places as appealing or varied, while students of history can learn much about the nation's heritage.

The following pages present some of the highlights of the forests. With more than twelve million acres to cover, no single book can describe all of the worthwhile features. Visitors to any of the forests will benefit by calling on the ranger stations, where representatives are happy to provide maps, brochures, and other information. Maps are particularly helpful because of the immensity of most of the forests and the remoteness of some of their attractions. This sense of remoteness that the forests offer leaves an enduring impression, welcome in an increasingly urban country. But much of the territory is quite rugged, and visitors should keep that in mind as they explore. ♠

Old hemlocks, some standing for 300 years or more, cling to a mountain slope in the George Washington National Forest in Virginia. Inaccessibility probably spared the stately trees from loggers in the early 1900s. When the trees fall from disease or age, resulting gaps allow sunlight to spur new growth. STEVEN Q. CROY

George Washington

N   A   T   I   O   N   A   L   F   O   R   E   S   T

Virginia treasure

In western Virginia, adjoining West Virginia, stand a series of high peaks perfect for escaping the most tenacious summer heat. Even when the Shenandoah Valley below is sweltering, Reddish Knob, Bother Knob, Flagpole Knob, and other nearby mountaintops welcome visitors with cool breezes. These crests also offer incomparable views of the George Washington National Forest, established in 1917. The George Washington—which shares a border on the south with Virginia's other national forest, the Jefferson—covers more than one million acres, dominated by mixed hardwoods. About eight million people travel to the George Washington each year, many of them drawn by panoramic views from the forest's high elevations. Located primarily in northwest Virginia, the George Washington also reaches into five West Virginia counties and is the only southern national forest with three different mountain ranges within its borders.

Along the western edge of the George Washington stretch the Allegheny Mountains, a long, ruffled line of summits interspersed with broad valleys. Much of the Allegheny range that lies in western Virginia falls within the George Washington. Stand atop one of the Allegheny knobs, look eastward across the broad Shenandoah Valley, and you see the Massanutten Mountains, running down the valley center. These are the mountains Confederate General Stonewall Jackson used so devastatingly well in a game of hide-and-seek with Federal troops during the Civil War. Farther still in the distance, behind the Massanutten, is another row of peaks, the Blue Ridge Mountains, which form the eastern boundary of the Shenandoah Valley.

Any of the Allegheny knobs is an ideal spot to begin a visit to the forest. In places, trails used by animals as much as hikers lead upward to summits through patches of hay-scented fern. Brushing against the waist-high plants that release a strong scent of freshly-mown fields is like being massaged by feathers. Near the ferns grow the fluffy white blooms of fly poison, the roots of which were once ground and used to keep pests away. Providing shade on the field edges are stately red oaks, gnarled by fierce winds and age.

Nearby are old stands of trees missed by loggers in the early 1900s. Some of the trees, marked by massive trunks, are 300 or more years old. Magnificent hemlocks grow beside black and yellow birch, tulip poplars, and oaks. The old trees' tops tend to be flattened and rounded, and their lower limbs have fallen away long ago. Interspersed among the living trees are the dead snags, where birds perch and other creatures make homes. When the big trees finally fall, weighted by age or disease, they often topple other trees, opening large gaps in the forest where sunlight streams through. Tender vegetation, much favored by wildlife, quickly springs up in these pockets. The forest floor is rich from the decay of the fallen giants, with doughy-soft slime mold sharing an uprooted trunk with shell fungi as big as a dinner plate. Salamanders, among the most abundant vertebates in the forest, also find a haven beneath the rotting wood.

Farther north, still in the Alleghenies, is another type of view atop a large rock outcrop sitting on Mill Mountain. Called the Big Schloss, German for "castle," the outcrop dominates the skyline for miles. A trail from Wolf Gap Campground reaches the rock top at 3,000 feet and continues on the long ridge beyond. Hearty mountain bikers enjoy the level sur-

Left: Fluffy blossoms of fly poison appear in open woods from June through July.
STEVEN Q. CROY
Above right: The red spikes of Indian paintbrush color open meadows.
STEVEN Q. CROY
Right: While the surrounding mountain soils are often thin, Virginia valleys are lush grazing grounds. FREDERICK D. ATWOOD

face of this high altitude trail, but to reach it must often push or carry their bikes in a strenuous climb. In late summer, the plump sweetness of wild blueberries also draws visitors. Just south of Reddish Knob lies the Wild Oak National Recreation Trail, a twenty-five-mile loop with elevations ranging from 1,600 to 4,351 feet. On Big Bald Knob, one of the trail's higher points, there is a wildlife clearing where mountain laurel show off their delicate pink and white flower cups in early summer. Look closely and you might find the footprints of bobcats. Some horseback riders use the trail, but grades are steep.

The Wild Oak and other trails make the George Washington especially popular among hikers. There are more than 900 miles of trails crisscrossing the forest, including sixty miles of the Appalachian Trail and sections of the Big Blue Trail which reaches far into Maryland. Some of the more adventurous hikers prefer bushwhacking, forging their own way in cross-country treks where there are no trails to follow. The George Washington's four wilderness areas, covering more than 32,000 acres, are favored ground for these hardy explorers.

For the more sedate, a leisurely drive along U. S. Route 250 cuts across the Alleghenies and can be especially pleasurable in the fall when the trees blaze different colors. The road provides access to Ramseys Draft Wilderness and also leads to the Confederate Breastworks where a short, one-third

mile interpretive trail informs visitors of the fierce Civil War struggles that enveloped the area.

Different types of recreational opportunities await visitors farther south in the Alleghenies near Covington at Lake Moomaw, a 2,500-acre lake twelve miles long. Sailing, skiing, fishing, or just cruising the lake in a canoe or other small boat are popular pastimes. Among the more unusual sights are deer standing waist-deep in water to graze on the lake bottom. Come close and the cautious deer may quickly thrust their heads up from below, forcing sheets of water to cascade from them like fountains.

Floating on Lake Moomaw is also a good way to observe the colorful mix of shale, limestone, and sandstone sedimentary rocks that dominate in the Alleghenies. The layers are well exposed in a bluff excavated to provide materials for a dam forming the

lake. Fishing in Lake Moomaw is excellent, with rainbow and brown trout weighing four to eight pounds. Ducks, geese, great blue herons, ospreys, even an occasional snowy egret and loon flock to the waters, attracted by the fish and by small islands made for them by the Forest Service. Floating nesting platforms for geese have also been installed and a handful of trees were intentionally girdled to provide snags where eagles prefer to perch. Several full-facility campgrounds hug the shoreline, with more planned. A primitive campground is accessible only by foot or boat.

Altogether, the George Washington has twenty-seven developed campgrounds and 3,190 acres of lakes and ponds. There are fees for the more developed facilities, while the more primitive ones are free. Near the border with West Virginia, Locust Springs Picnic Area offers one of several entrance ways into the

Left: *The Blue Ridge Mountains are one of three mountain ranges within the George Washington National Forest.* STEVEN Q. CROY
Above: *Salamanders, including this Cow Knob, are among the forest's predominant residents.* STEVEN Q. CROY

FALCON
PRESS®

BUSINESS REPLY MAIL

FIRST-CLASS MAIL PERMIT NO 80 HELENA MT

POSTAGE WILL BE PAID BY ADDRESSEE

FALCON PRESS PUBLISHING CO
PO BOX 1718
HELENA MT   59624-9948

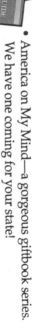
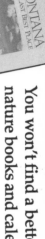

UNWELCOME GYPSIES

An unusually high number of dead trees stand forlornly in the George Washington National Forest. Stripped of all leaves, they look like skeletons, limbs pointing eerily this way and that. Sadly, more trees are likely to join their ranks as an insatiable predator, the gypsy moth, eats its way through the forest.

Introduced into Massachusetts in the 1860s by a French scientist as part of a silk production experiment, the moth soon escaped captivity and gradually multiplied and migrated over the Northeast. Only within the past few years has it reached the South—but already the devastation is enormous.

Gypsy moth larvae lead to a tree's destruction by eating its leaves. The tree responds by producing another set of leaves, sapping its resources. While some trees can withstand the stress, others can't, and die because they become more susceptible to disease, drought, and other insects. Many of the stricken trees are logged in salvage operations, making up a growing percentage of the thirty-six million board feet harvested in the forest annually. Other trees fall and fertilize forest soils.

Moth larvae prefer oaks, but will attack a wide range of vegetation. By 1990 they had ravaged an estimated 126,000 acres in the George Washington. About 14,000 acres of those trees died as a result. The Forest Service is fighting back, trying methods to curb the moths, including a naturally-occurring bacteria and limited use of insecticides. Scientists are also using a virus and a fungus against the insects.

If the gypsy moth cannot be stopped, the George Washington National Forest of the future is likely to have far fewer oaks—perhaps a third less. The oak decline will allow red maples, yellow poplars, and other trees less susceptible to the moths to grow, but how the loss will affect wildlife—especially deer, turkey, and other species that eat acorns—is another cause of concern.

Above: Trees, defoliated by gypsy moths, respond with new growth. JOHN SHAW.
Right: The gypsy moth caterpillar causes immense losses of trees through its voracious appetite. The moths escaped from an 1860s experiment.
FRED CRAMER

Laurel Fork area where elevations reach higher than 4,000 feet. Laurel Fork is rife with beaver ponds, and a stealthy visitor can spot the creatures floating near their lodges in late afternoon or early morning. Mossy bogs and a fringe of red spruce, hemlock, and white pine surround the ponds. Wildlife here is abundant, particularly white-tailed deer. Or you may spot a gray fox bounding away with a furtive look back over his shoulder.

Laurel Fork is home to more than thirty animals and plants considered rare in Virginia, including the snowshoe hare and northern flying squirrel. Overall, the George Washington hosts some 250 plants and animals considered rare, threatened, or endangered in Virginia. At least forty-eight areas in the forest are managed for the protection and enhancement of these species.

Many visitors to the George Washington are ushered in through the scenic Blue Ridge Parkway, managed by the National Park Service. The parkway winds through the Blue Ridge Mountains and travels across the forest for about sixty miles, giving access to some of the George Washington's most popular attractions. Among them is Crabtree Falls, where five cascades tumble more than a thousand feet. A twisting, three-mile trail leads to the top of the falls, with three observation platforms and several benches along the way. Another sitting area at the top offers a fine view of the forest. Caution is advised here: at least twenty-one people who strayed out over the rocks away from the trail have died as a result.

Large hemlocks and other old trees hover over the path. The bark of some of the hemlocks has a pinkish tinge as if the trees were sunburned. The culprit is a wooly aphid infestation, just one of the predators loose in the forest and attacking the trees (see sidebar story). The giant boulders along the trail are typical of the

---

Sherando Lake has the biggest swimming beach in the George Washington National Forest. Located near the Blue Ridge Parkway, the twenty-four acre lake has a small island near its center, popular among swimmers. SHOFFNER

metamorphic and igneous rocks found in this part of the Blue Ridge, which are some of the oldest mountains in the East.

Another spot on the Blue Ridge Parkway leads from the Mine Bank to a trailhead into St. Mary's Wilderness. Unfortunately, hiking into the wilderness has become so popular that the main trail, which follows the St. Mary's River, has at times become overcrowded. Some camp-

Above: Solitary trout fishing in cold mountain streams is one of the many recreation possibilities in the forest. Anglers also take advantage of lakes stocked with bass. A Virginia fishing license and National Forest stamp are required. BILL LEA

Left: Only an observant eye would notice the deathly-still gray tree frog camouflaged in its woodland habitat. Elongated fingers with a tenacious grasp help the frog navigate up and down its tree perch. STEVEN Q. CROY

WARWICK MANSION: A LOOK BACK

Stepping onto the front porch of Warwick Mansion is like moving back through time. Wealthy planters across the antebellum South favored residences like this as they embraced Greek Revival style in homage to classical architecture. The mansion, built in 1848, was largely the work of slaves, who made the hundreds of red bricks forming the walls, which are more than a foot thick.

A private permittee, in cooperation with the George Washington National Forest, which owns the property, leases the house and is rehabilitating it as a bed and breakfast inn. Guests will stay amid period furnishings painstakingly collected. Four white columns support the graceful roof, which is topped by a widow's walk, an observation point for the once enormous estate, parts of which will once again be a working farm. The view also includes three log cabins, which appear to be as old as the house, but are really recent additions for a Hollywood-produced movie starring Jodie Foster and Richard Gere.

People have occupied the site near the Jackson River for 9,000 years, and some of their artifact traces, uncovered by archeologists, will be displayed in a Forest Service interpretive exhibit in the area. Whether the mansion's reputed friendly ghost will also display itself is less certain.

---

ing restrictions are the result, so check with the ranger office before venturing on an overnight stay. Hiking away from the trail is difficult because of the rugged terrain and steep quartzite cliffs. Weekdays are the least crowded throughout the forest, but for those seeking a more solitary experience, try the Henry Lanum Jr. Trail, a five-mile circuit that climbs Mount Pleasant and the Pompey Mountains, both more than 4,000 feet high.

Another recreation area not far from the parkway is Sherando Lake, offering full-service camping and the largest swimming beach in the forest. Bathers enjoy swimming to an island near the center of the twenty-four-acre lake, while an adjacent lake is popular for fishing. The combined bathhouse and visitor center was built in the 1930s by the Civilian Conservation Corps, one of their many projects in the forest. They used local stone to build this and other structures, which stand as a testament to their skill and labor. Every year, surviving CCC members who worked as young men to build the roads, dams, and buildings in the George Washington return to Sherando Lake with their families for a reunion. A boulder near the bathhouse is inscribed with a commemoration to their accomplishments.

The gateway to the George Washington's other mountain range, the Massanutten, is the Massanutten Visitor Center, where guidebooks, a video library, and brochures are available about the forest. There are several interpretive trails close by, including the Lion's

Tale Trail for the blind and the Story Book Trail, accessible to wheelchairs. While they are specially designed for those with disabilities, both trails are also popular with other visitors.

Also popular in the Massanutten is the Elizabeth Furnace Recreation Area with camping, interpretive paths about early iron mining, and a trail to Signal Knob where Confederate soldiers once spied on Union troops. History buffs will enjoy hiking the twenty-four-mile Sherman Gap Loop, built partly on the escape route General George Washington planned to use during the Revolutionary War if the tide turned against him at Yorktown. Nearby, visitors enjoy fishing, canoeing, and tubing on the South Fork of the Shenandoah River, just a few of the many opportunities for enjoying the George Washington National Forest. ♠

Five cascades tumble down more than 1,000 feet at Crabtree Falls. A three-mile trail leads to the top. STEVE SOLUM

George Washington
NATIONAL FOREST DIRECTORY

POINTS OF INTEREST

Massanutten Visitors Center On U. S. Highway 211 not far from New Market, Virginia, and Interstate Highway 81. A good place for an introduction to the forest with guidebooks, maps, videos, and other interpretive materials.

Reddish Knob West of Harrisonburg on Forest Service Route 85. With an elevation of 4,397 feet, the knob offers excellent views of the surrounding mountains and the Shenandoah Valley.

Lake Moomaw 2,530-acre lake in southwest portion of the forest not far from West Virginia. The lake is about twenty miles north of Interstate 64 and about twenty-four miles south and west of Hot Springs, Virginia. Camping, fishing, boating, hiking, and picnicking are popular.

Crabtree Falls Near Blue Ridge Parkway on State Road 56. A short walk leads to the base of the falls. A three-mile trail leads to the top of a series of five falls.

WILDERNESS AREAS

St. Mary's 9,835 acres on east side of the forest in Blue Ridge Mountains. Quartzite cliffs, a trout-filled river with a picturesque waterfall, and remnants of old mines.

Ramseys Draft 6,518 acres of mountainous country with elevations about 4000 feet. Located in western part of the forest, the wilderness includes areas where virgin trees still grow. Access by seven trailheads.

Rich Hole 6,450 acres in Allegheny Mountains in southwest portion of the forest. Undiscovered by most, with opportunities for solitude.

Rough Mountain 9,300 acres close to Rich Hole Wilderness.

RECREATION OPPORTUNITIES

Hiking and Riding More than 900 miles of trails including more than sixty miles of Appalachian National Scenic Trail. Horseback riding popular on some of these trails, but prohibited on the Appalachian Trail.

Camping Twenty-seven developed campgrounds. Reservations allowed at some full-service facilities.

Swimming Six lakes with seven beaches.

Fishing Opportunities in many lakes and streams for trout, smallmouth and largemouth bass, channel catfish, and bluegill. State license and National Forest stamp required.

Hunting Deer, turkey, ruffed grouse, squirrel, and other game. National Forest hunting stamp and state license required.

Shooting Four rifle ranges spaced across the forest near Covington, Staunton, and Bath Alum, Va., and near Brandywine, W. Va.

Off-Road Vehicles Two routes, Peters Mill Run and Taskers Gap, are off Virginia Highway 675, southeast of Edinburg. Neal Run, accessible to the disabled, is west of Warm Springs, Va., in Bath County. Rocky Run is thirteen miles west of Harrisonburg on U. S. Hwy. 33.

Canoeing and Rafting South Fork of Shenandoah River is popular, with boat rentals available.

Scenic Drives Highlands Scenic Tour is a twenty-mile loop in the southwest part of the forest, accessible from Interstate 64. Elevations range from about 1,000 feet to more than 3,000 feet. Also popular, especially in fall, is U. S. Highway 250 which travels near Ramseys Draft Wilderness.

ADMINISTRATIVE OFFICES

Forest Headquarters Harrison Plaza, 101 N. Main St., P. O. Box 233, Harrisonburg, VA 22801 (703) 433-2491

Deerfield Ranger District W. Beverley St., Staunton, VA 24401 (703) 885-8028 or 885-8029

Dry River Ranger District 112 N. River Road, Bridgewater VA 22812 (703) 828-2591

James River Ranger District 810-A Madison Ave., Covington, VA 24426 (703) 962-2214

Lee Ranger District Windsor Knit Road, Route 4, Box 515, Edinburg, VA 22824 (703) 984-4101 or 984-4102

Pedlar Ranger District 2424 Magnolia Ave., Buena Vista, VA 24416 (703) 261-6105 or 261-6106 or 261-6107

Warm Springs Ranger District Route 2, Box 30, Hot Springs, VA 24445 (703) 839-2521 or 839-2442

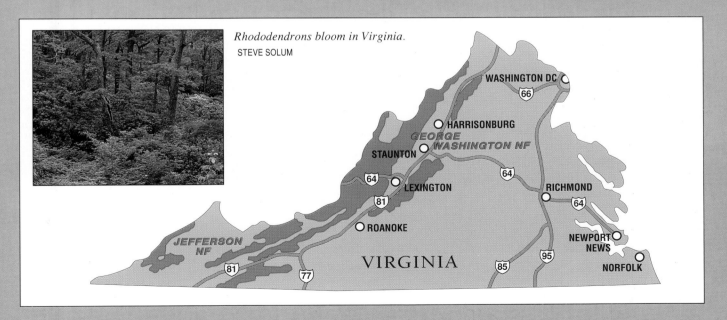

Rhododendrons bloom in Virginia.
STEVE SOLUM

The high Appalachian Mountain balds of southwest Virginia offer wonderfully crisp fresh air, unimpeded views of the undulating landscape, and, at the right time of year, profuse wildflower displays. These yellow blooms of ragwort can begin unfolding as early as April, depending on temperatures and elevations. STEVE SOLUM

Jefferson

N   A   T   I   O   N   A   L   F   O   R   E   S   T

Rounded peaks and quiet coves

Quiet valleys with small farms dotting the hillsides are nestled one after another below the rounded Appalachian Mountains that make up much of the Jefferson National Forest. Mostly slow-going, narrow roads wind through this tranquil landscape in southwestern Virginia, dictating a leisurely pace of travel and providing a chance to enjoy great beauty with little effort. Sky-blue blossoms of chicory decorate the valley roadsides in summer like a necklace with many strands, while the tall, white flower spikes of black cohosh reach out from the borders of mountain woods. A roly-poly groundhog, or woodchuck, seems to be nibbling near the asphalt at every turn, while the persistent songs of vireos fill the air.

In autumn, fiery reds of maples and oaks mix with the golden yellows of poplars and hickories and the deep greens of spruce and fir, the out-of-place remnants from the last glacial retreat thousands of years ago. This extravagant color show draws visitors from miles away to the Jefferson, where far fewer venture in winter when deep snow can bury fields and overlay peaks. For some, however, the coldest months are favored because snow can change the many hiking trails into smooth gliding paths for cross country skis.

The forest's namesake, Thomas Jefferson, third president of the United States and an avid Virginia farmer and nature lover, no doubt would be pleased to see how these 705,192 acres have been nursed back to health since the forest was established in 1936. Like so many of the eastern mountains, this stretch of the Appalachians was stripped nearly bare of trees, but scars of that era are hard to find today. More than 57,000 acres are set aside in eleven wilderness areas, where human impact is strictly minimized. And while the rest of the Jefferson is a working forest, with about fifty percent of it available for an annual harvest of thirty-three million board feet of timber, sites and cutting methods are chosen to minimize impact. Indeed, healthy forest soils contribute to the 315 billion gallons of useable water the Jefferson produces annually. And for reasons not yet fully understood, forest stands of Fraser fir appear undamaged so far from the balsam wooly aphid, an insect that injects a deadly secretion into trees while feeding below the bark. The aphids have devastated Fraser firs elsewhere. Consequently, cones for reproducing seedlings from the

Jefferson's healthy trees are in big demand among commercial growers. Further uses of the forest include cattle grazing and limited oil, gas, and coal production.

Like most national forests in the South, the Jefferson is not one big sweep of contiguous acreage, but a collection of lands intermingled with private property. Extending 218 miles from the James River on the north to the Kentucky state line on the south, the forest even includes some ground in West Virginia and Kentucky, but the bulk lies within Virginia. The forest's size and dispersal require five separate ranger districts for management, while yet another team oversees the Jefferson's special 115,000 acres designated expressly for public enjoyment—the Mount Rogers National Recreation Area (MRNRA).

Starting at the Tennessee border, the MRNRA reaches eastward for about sixty-five miles in a narrow finger, enveloping both low ground laced with clear, cold streams, eighty miles of which are stocked with trout, and high country offering spectacular vistas. Hikers, however, should not expect a panoramic reward when they reach the top of Mount Rogers, Virginia's highest peak at 5,729 feet. Instead, make the ascent for the pleasure of the climb because trees mostly shroud the view. Others more inclined to reach great heights while sitting can drive Virginia's highest road up Whitetop Mountain, a grassy bald, where the view is unimpeded for miles. A prime vantage point on Whitetop is Buzzard Rock, an outcrop on the Appalachian Trail, fifty-eight miles of which pass through the MRNRA. Visitors perch on Buzzard Rock to watch spectacular sunsets and migrating raptors catching the updrafts swirling around the mountain. The air, it seems, is always stirring on Whitetop, from

Mount Rogers, Virginia's highest peak at 5,729 feet, is the centerpiece for the Mount Rogers National Recreation Area, designated expressly for public enjoyment. Hikers, equestrians, and visitors who appreciate stunning beauty all favor the region. STEVE Q. CROY

WHERE THE WHISTLE BLEW

Green Cove Railroad Depot and store, once the focus of community life in a small rural enclave, is now a Forest Service visitor center.
SHARYN KANE/
RICHARD KEETON

Green Cove is a tiny mountain valley community in southwest Virginia. For years, a simple white clapboard building was the focal point for commerce and conversation in Green Cove. This was where the sick went to buy remedies; where telegrams and mail were sent and collected; where voters cast their ballots; and where passengers caught the outbound train. Farm women brought their eggs and butter to swap for needles and thread or whatever else they needed. And when nothing much else was happening, everybody in town was likely to gather around the old pot-bellied stove to swap stories and pass the time.

Built around 1916, the Green Cove Railroad Depot and General Store is now part of the Mount Rogers National Recreation Area. The last train passed through years ago, and the general store eventually closed down, too. Forest Service archeologists and others are working to restore the building, now a visitor center staffed part-time by Green Cove volunteers. Appropriately, the Virginia Creeper Trail passes by the depot, where visitors can stop in for maps and brochures about the forest and catch a glimpse of a bygone era. Pink powder puffs, starched collars, and old patent medicines rest on the shelves, undisturbed for decades. The faint odor of oil used to clean the wood floor is in the air, and one can easily imagine that the old Virginia Creeper whistle is blowing around the bend.

---

summer's cooling breezes to winter's bracing winds.

The grazing of 120 wild ponies helps maintain another of the MRNRA's grassy balds, Pine Mountain. Descendants from a herd released years ago, the lively ponies occasionally approach visitors in search of a handout. A veterinarian keeps an eye on the animals' health, while the herd size is kept low through an annual auction the last weekend of September, when about twenty ponies are sold as pets. Another group of the MRNRA's inhabitants, eighteen species of salamanders, are much less visible because of their relatively small size, preference for hidden spots, and nocturnal habits. Nonetheless, salamanders, including species classified as sensitive such as the shovel-nosed, pygmy, Weller's, and Yonahlossee, are important consider-

A herd of 120 wild ponies lives in the Jefferson National Forest. Many of them are friendly and make ideal pets. An annual fall auction of selected ponies helps keep the herd small. PHOTO COURTESY OF USDA FOREST SERVICE - ROBERT L. McKINNEY

Nocturnal opossums are rarely seen in daylight. A female opossum can have as many as sixteen offspring at a time. FRED CRAMER

ations in forest management.

Unlike many public recreation spots, much of the MRNRA is often uncrowded, even under-used. Campsites are refreshingly tree-shaded on the hottest afternoons, with the added bonus of a fourteen-acre lake for swimming, boating, and fishing at Beartree Campground, the largest of seven designated camping areas. Yet even in midsummer, visitors can arrive late in the day and still have a good chance of finding a vacancy, except on major summer holidays. Horseback riders, however, are more likely to encounter crowds at most camping spots set aside for them because of the popularity of the Virginia Highlands Horse Trail, which can attract 300 riders on weekends and holidays. The heavy use is cause for concern among forest

FIERY FURNACES

The searing heat and sooty smoke were horrendous when iron furnaces burned in Virginia, starting with the American Revolution and continuing until after the Civil War. A scattering of the furnaces, most with pyramid rock towers intact and a few with wood sheds attached, can still be found. In the Jefferson National Forest, for example, much of the stone structure is left of Roaring Run Furnace, listed on the National Register of Historic Places.

Plentiful iron ore and limestone, chief ingredients for producing pig iron, made Virginia ideal for an industry that also demanded plenty of timber for charcoal—burned to smelt iron ore—and water power to turn wheels that operated fire bellows. Skilled men called "colliers" burned felled trees slowly around-the-clock for two weeks in a careful arrangement up to ten feet tall and twenty feet wide

Left: A Forest Service interpreter explains how Roaring Run Furnace operated. SHARYN KANE/ RICHARD KEETON

Below: Iron furnace ruins dot the countryside. SHARYN KANE/RICHARD KEETON

beneath a blanket of dirt. The resultant charcoal was then taken to the furnace, where it was mixed with the ore and limestone and loaded into the furnace by dumping the mixture down the top of the rock pyramid to the matrix below. The furnace was built next to a hillside so workers could reach its opening. The mix was raised to a scorching temperature of 2,600 degrees, and kept burning, often by slaves, until it formed liquid iron.

Then the molten liquid was released to flow into the shed where it poured into a series of shallow trench molds dug in sand off one main row. The molds reminded an onlooker of a mother pig and her sucklings, which is how the term "pig iron" came to be.

managers, who are considering ways to offset the impact without hindering visitor enjoyment. Riders seeking more solitude, for example, are encouraged to use trails on the less-visited eastern section of the recreation area. Similarly, visitors interested in exploring a wilderness are directed to Little Dry Run Wilderness rather than the more heavily used Lewis Fork and Little Wilson Creek wilderness areas.

Another highlight of the recreation area is the Virginia Creeper National Recreation Trail, which follows an old railroad bed starting in the town of Abingdon, then passes through the MRNRA for about eighteen miles before it ends at the North Carolina border. Virginia Creeper was the unofficial name for the steam-powered logging train that ran through the forest starting in the early 1900s. The steep Appalachians reportedly slowed the engine to a crawl, allowing riders to hop off to pick blackberries, then climb back on with ease. Coursing through a narrow gorge, the trail crosses over many short bridges and a dramatic, 500-foot-long wooden trestle suspended 120 feet above Whitetop Laurel Creek. The trail is open to non-motorized mountain bikes, horses, hikers, and skiers, and briefly shares ground with the Appalachian Trail, best-known of the more than 300 miles of trails in the MRNRA.

Appalachian Trail hikers making the entire trek from Georgia to Maine often arrange their journey to arrive in Damascus, Virginia, near the Jefferson in mid-May for the Appalachian Trail Days. Billed as "the friendliest town on the trail," Damascus stages a square dance, barbeque, and parade for hikers, who are invited to

camp in town during festivities. Residents don period costumes and the strains of lively music abound in a celebration of spring and neighborliness. Summer visitors to the MRNRA may also encounter a costumed character or two, along with string musicians, who perform in free campground programs sponsored by the Forest Service. A salty old character named Wilburn Waters, portrayed by interpretive specialist Robert McKinney in a flowing white wig, regales audiences with tales about bears and other aspects of rugged mountain life in the nineteenth century, while the musicians are students from the tiny Mount Rogers Combined School, the smallest K-12 school in the

The trunks of red spruce trees provided resin for early chewing gum, while young twigs from the evergreens were boiled with sugar and flavorings to make spruce beer.
STEVEN Q. CROY

state. Calling themselves the Albert Hash Memorial Old-time String Music Band, the youngsters play instruments and sing songs long cherished in the mountains.

Besides the MRNRA, the Jefferson offers many more places of interest, several of them designed expressly for easy accessibility by the disabled. Fenwick Mines Trail near New Castle, for example, is a new 3,700-foot trail suitable for wheelchairs. An overlook for wildlife viewing is built over wetlands, and there is also a fishing pond and picnic area with specially designed tables. Extensive work has also been done recently to make Bark Camp Lake in southwestern

Virginia accessible with wheelchair ramps and paved walkways.

Nearly 900 people may visit another favorite spot on a summer day, Cascades Recreation Area, near Pembroke. The main attraction is a sixty-six-foot waterfall pouring over an impressive rock staircase. The Cascades National Recreation Trail, an easy to moderately difficult four-mile round trip, is an enjoyable hike to the falls. Fishing and picnicking are also popular.

Many of the forest's recreation areas have streams or creeks with cool, fresh water favored by anglers and swimmers. One of the most picturesque spots lies near the northern tip of the Jefferson—Cave Mountain Lake. The lake has a popular sand beach and adjacent campground nestled amid large pines and hardwoods. High Knob Recreation Area, near Norton, also has a swimming beach on a four-acre, cold water lake. A campground nearby features a trail to the top of High Knob, where an observation tower overlooks the forest from 4,160 feet. This and many other peaks in the forest provide ideal vantage points to enjoy the Jefferson's rich array of woods and valleys. ♣

Jefferson
NATIONAL FOREST DIRECTORY

POINTS OF INTEREST

Mount Rogers National Recreation Area 117,000 acres of some of Virginia's best recreation sites and scenery, including the state's highest peak, Mount Rogers, 5,729 feet. Ranger office and visitor center on Route 16, seven miles south of Marion, offer maps, brochures, displays, and guide books highlighting the area.

Green Cove Visitor Center On Virginia Route 600, a mile south of Route 58, stands an old railroad depot and general store with original contents. Weekend volunteers provide maps and brochures in this recent addition to Mount Rogers National Recreation Area.

Roaring Run Furnace and Picnic Area Features historic iron furnace in a wooded setting near a stream and wooded picnic grounds in the New Castle Ranger District.

Highlands Gateway Visitor Center Brand new location at the Factory Merchants Mall, located off I-81, Exit 80. Educational and informative displays. Open year-round.

Natural Bridge Visitor Center Excellent pictorial displays about the forest and brochures and guides. Open year-round except winter season in Natural Bridge, Va.

Settlers Museum of Southwest Virginia A "living history" village being recreated near Groseclose on the Jefferson National Forest. A one-room school house from 1894 and a visitor center are open, with more exhibits planned.

Cascades Recreation Area Includes dramatic, sixty-six-foot waterfall, trails, and picnic area, near Blacksburg.

WILDERNESS AREAS

Peters Mountain 3,326 acres near Blacksburg.

Mountain Lake 10,753 acres, near Blacksburg, contains only natural lake in western Virginia.

James River Face 8,703 acres in northern part of forest.

Thunder Ridge 2,797 acres in northern part of forest.

Little Dry Run 3,400 acres in Mount Rogers National Recreation Area.

Little Wilson Creek 3,885 acres in Mount Rogers National Recreation Area.

Lewis Fork 5,730 acres in Mount Rogers National Recreation Area.

Barbours Creek 5,700 acres near New Castle.

Shawvers Run 3,570 acres near New Castle.

Beartown 6,375 acres near Wytheville.

Kimberling Creek 5,580 acres near Wytheville.

RECREATIONAL OPPORTUNITIES

Hiking and Riding Over 1,000 miles of trails, including 300 miles of Appalachian National Scenic Trail. Difficulty ranges from short, easy loops to strenuous mountain climbs. Virginia Creeper Trail is multi-use and thirty-seven miles long, much of it through Mount Rogers National Recreation Area. Voted one of "America's Ten Best Bicycle Trails" in 1992. Virginia Highlands Horse Trail, sixty-eight miles, also passes through MRNRA. A new sixty-mile horse trail is also located within the Glenwood Ranger District on the north end of the forest.

Camping Twenty-two developed camping areas and excellent opportunities for backcountry camping.

Scenic Drives Mount Rogers Scenic Byway is in two sections totaling about fifty-five miles. From Troutdale, take Virginia 603 west to U.S. 58, a twenty-three-mile stretch. From Damascus, take U.S. 58 east to Volney, thirty-two miles.

Big Walker Mountain Scenic Byway Passes for about sixteen miles in Bland and Wythe Counties. Access from Interstate 77 and 81 at Wytheville.

Blue Ridge Parkway Cuts through northern part of the forest next to James River Face Wilderness.

Boating, Kayaking, and Tubing Small boats on forest lakes and kayaks and inner tubes on streams and creeks are popular, although water levels can drop significantly in creeks and streams in summer.

Hunting Deer, ruffed grouse, turkey, and other species. Forest stamp required and license from Virginia Game and Fish Department.

Fishing Both native and stocked trout plentiful in numerous mountain streams, stocked in spring and summer. Check with local wildlife officials for special regulations on catch and release or other limits. Forest stamp and state license required.

Cross-Country Skiing Snowfall greatly variable. No designated trails, but miles of pathways on hiking and riding trails and primitive roads. Rentals and ski wax available in some sporting goods stores along interstate highway corridors.

Feathercamp Motorcycle Trails More than ten miles of riding in Mount Rogers National Recreation Area. Additional seasonal trails also open. Contact ranger for details.

Pine Mountain Jeep Trail Three-mile, four-wheel-drive road starts west of Troutdale. Otherwise, off-road vehicles are prohibited throughout the forest.

Mountain Bicycling Allowed on forest service roads and some trails, with restrictions. Prohibited in all wilderness areas. Check with ranger for details.

ADMINISTRATIVE OFFICES

Forest Headquarters 210 Franklin Rd., SW Roanoke, VA 24001 (703) 982-6270

Mount Rogers National Recreation Area Route 1, Box 303, Marion, VA 24354 (703) 783-5196

Blacksburg Ranger District 3089 Pandapas Pond Road, Blacksburg, VA 24060 (703) 552-4641

Clinch Ranger District 9416 Darden Drive, Wise, VA 24293 (703) 328-2931

Glenwood Ranger District P. O. Box 10, Natural Bridge Station, VA 24579 (703) 291-2188

New Castle Ranger District P. O. Box 246, New Castle, VA 24147 (703) 864-5195

Wythe Ranger District 1625 West Lee Highway, Wytheville, VA 24382 (703) 228-5551

Virginia beauty: lacy dogwood petals unfurl in spring. THOMAS R. FLETCHER

The South Fork of the Cumberland River courses through land that drew pioneers like Daniel Boone westward in search of wild, untamed country. The Daniel Boone National Forest has 500 miles of streams flowing within its boundaries, as well as sweeping cliffs that once provided shelter for early people. J.C. LEACOCK

Daniel Boone

N A T I O N A L   F O R E S T

Pioneer spirit

Tales of Kentucky and Daniel Boone are stitched side by side in the fabric of truth and legend about pioneer America, making it only fitting that Kentucky's single national forest is named for the buckskin-clad frontiersman.

The 670,000 acres of the Daniel Boone National Forest, established in 1937, are divided into two principal sections. The first extends like a pointed finger from the Tennessee border northward through the eastern Kentucky mountains. The second part, the Redbird Ranger District, is a dispersed collection of lands farther east. Taken together, they include some of the state's most rugged scenery, characterized by steep slopes, narrow valleys, and more than 3,400 miles of cliffline. Oaks, hickories, poplars, and other hardwoods predominate, and, with yellow pines, account for most of the thirty-nine million board feet of timber harvested in a year.

Daniel Boone was far from the first to travel this territory west of the Allegheny Mountains, but he is clearly the best-remembered of early adventurers. French explorers preceded him by nearly 100 years and Native Americans by thousands more than that. Word of the region's plentiful game, water, and verdant land reached Boone as a young man in North Carolina, and he became determined to see the place for himself. When he made his first trip in 1769, he understood why the Shawnee and Cherokee Indians had fought so many wars over the region that it became known as the "Dark and Bloody Ground." Several years after his first visit, Boone returned with his family and a small group of others to establish a settlement that became Fort Boonesborough, today a state park.

Boone was an inveterate explorer and saw much of the forest bearing his name. The Sheltowee Trace, a national recreation trail, follows his path across the length of the forest for 257 miles from Tennessee to the northern forest border. "Sheltowee," which means "big turtle," was the name given to Boone by Black Fish, a Shawnee chief. Black Fish and his followers captured Boone, along with twenty-seven others, as they made salt at a salt springs in 1778. In the days before refrigeration, salt was essential to meat preservation and the men risked their lives to get it. Boone somehow won the Indian chief over and was adopted by him into the tribe. Boone eventually escaped and he

and the other settlers at Fort Boonesborough successfully fought off a long siege by the chief and his warriors.

The Sheltowee Trace, marked with a turtle symbol, ventures through some of the most visually stunning parts of the forest and provides access to many recreation sites. Deep canyons, narrow ridgetops, water features, and striking rimrock cliffs make the journey varied and challenging. Frequent access points along the way allow both through hikers and day visitors to enjoy the trail, which has many spurs to other paths. Primarily a foot trail, parts of the course are also open to horses and off-road vehicles. All of the trail, except parts passing through Clifty Wilderness and the Red River Gorge Geological Area, is open to mountain bicycles, as are many forest roads.

Starting from the north near Morehead, the Sheltowee Trace moves south towards Cave Run Lake, one of the three largest impoundments in the forest. Overall, there are a dozen lakes within the Daniel Boone or adjacent to its boundaries, and 1,200 miles of streams. A dam on the Licking River, named by pioneers for its nearness to a salt source, forms Cave Run Lake. The lake meanders for 8,270 acres and is famous for near-record size muskellunge, as well as good populations of largemouth bass, bluegill, crappie, and catfish. Giant Canada geese live year-round along the shore, one of more than 100 bird species found in the forest. In winter, fish-eating osprey and bald eagles may be seen near the lake.

The excellent fishing is attributed in part to timber deliberately left standing as the area was flooded by the U. S. Army Corps of Engineers, builders of the lake. The submerged trees provide habitat attractive to fish, but also pose hazards to unwary boaters, who should be on the lookout for signs identifying these areas. Windsurfing and sailing are popular in the gentle breezes that waft over Cave Run Lake, where several times a year a local sailing association holds colorful regattas. Visitors can try their hands at navigating the

Left: Lovely wild trillium blossoms sprout from the damp, mossy soils along stream banks in the Daniel Boone. BILL LEA
Above Right: The brilliant red plumage and distinctive crest of the male northern cardinal set him apart. F. D. ATWOOD
Right: Sky Bridge, stretching for seventy-five feet, is one of numerous sandstone arches in the forest. ADAM JONES

many coves in houseboats, pontoons, and jon boats rented at two marinas open year-round. Concession-aires also rent fishing and water skiing equipment.

The Morehead District Ranger Office and Visitor Center is located just north of the lake and offers exhibits and information about the forest. Nearby is Twin Knobs, one of two large recreation areas on opposite shores, both with campgrounds, swimming beaches, and hiking trails. Twin Knobs covers 700 acres, while Zilpo Recreation Area on the south shore occupies over 350 acres on the edge of a wooded peninsula. The Ziplo Recreation Area marks the end of the nine-mile national scenic byway (Zilpo Road or Forest Road 918). A smaller, third campground, Claylick, is more remote and accessible only by boat.

The byway has several overlooks and interpretive signs. A ridgetop road, it passes through the Pioneer Weapons Hunting Area. Spur trails from the Sheltowee Trace also lead into the 7,480-acre special section where hunters can use only longbow, crossbow, and black-powder rifles. The restrictions were imposed in 1962 to allow white-tailed deer and turkey populations to increase. The Tater Knob fire lookout tower along the byway overlooks the Pioneer Weapons Area and has been restored to provide panoramic views again as it did for fifty years.

History buffs will also enjoy another recreation area, Clear Creek Campground, located near the start of the byway on Highway 129. The rock base of a pig iron blast furnace built in 1839 is preserved at the site, one of many spots where the industry operated in the forest. The cut stone stack originally was forty feet tall. Iron made at the furnace, which ceased production in 1875, was used mostly for railway car wheels. A better-preserved furnace is located farther south at the Cottage Furnace Picnic Area on Forest Road 227 near Clay City.

Iron ore is only one of the rich deposits found in the Kentucky hills. There are more than fifty oil and gas leases in the forest and one active coal lease. Low coal prices and restrictions in the Clean Air Act are factors in reduced coal mining, which has long existed on the Daniel Boone. The Redbird District is particularly productive for natural gas wells.

Continuing south, the Sheltowee Trace cuts through the heart of Red River Gorge Geological Area, a natural masterpiece of sculpted rock spread over 25,662 acres. About half of the gorge was set aside as the Clifty Wilderness in 1985. More than 200 major sandstone arches and hundreds of rockshelters are found in this gorge, the largest concentration of these geological phenomena in the East. They are the stalwart remnants after seventy million years of wind and water eroded weaker rocks. Since prehistoric times, people have sought refuge in the rockshelters created by cliff overhangs, and these shallow recesses are the focus of

great archeological interest. Visitors are urged to avoid disturbing them.

The Sky Bridge is one of the most spectacular arches. Stretching for seventy-five feet along the top of a thin ridge, the arch provides a sweeping view of the gorge. This and many other highlights of the area can be enjoyed on a thirty-mile driving loop with scenic overlooks. Within the loop off the Mountain Parkway is the Gladie Historic Site and Information Station on State Route 715. Displays about early logging and farm life are featured in a restored 1884 log cabin, with available maps and brochures about the forest and other local places of interest. In fall, craftspeople demonstrate old-time skills like sorghum making and apple butter cooking.

Besides the Sheltowee Trace NRT, the Red River Gorge National Recreation Trail explores the area in a thirty-six-mile system of loop paths. Walking is the best way to view the tremendously varied array of plant life. There are more than 750 different flowering plants and 170 species of moss in the Clifty Wilderness alone, as well as fifteen plant species considered sensitive or endangered. Hikers may also see some of the forty-six species of mammals in the forest, including mink and red and gray foxes. Day visitors are less likely to encounter any of the many bat species in the forest, which provides crucial habitat to the endangered Indiana

and Virginia Big-eared bats. Protecting caves where the bats live is one of the Forest Service's leading resource management goals.

Canoeing and rafting are popular in the gorge on the Red River, a state designated wild river and one of seven waterways in the forest being considered for designation as federal wild and scenic rivers. Experienced canoeists often begin their trips in the whitewater sections in the upper reaches of the river's course through the gorge. The middle section is much tamer and suitable for beginners, while the lower stretch is generally too clogged for enjoyable floating. Usually, the Red River is navigable from late December through late May.

Laurel River Lake is the major recreation site in the southern half of the forest and like Cave Run Lake features marinas, hiking trails, and campgrounds, including two for boaters only. The Sheltowee Trace skirts the western stretch of the lake and intersects shorter trails leading to recreation spots near the water. After Laurel River Lake, the Sheltowee Trace travels south and west through the rest of the forest towards Tennessee. The 5,600-acre Laurel River Lake is known for exceptionally clean water and good catches of rainbow trout. West of Laurel River Lake there is another body of water, Lake Cumberland, formed by the waters of the Cumberland River. About 2,840 of

Left: Gladie Historic Site and Information Station is a restored 1884 log cabin. Featuring displays on early logging and farm life. ADAM JONES
Right: Professional outfitters guide seasonal float trips down the Cumberland River. ADAM JONES

the enormous lake's 63,000 acres are in the forest. Two campgrounds and a marina serve this part of Lake Cumberland. Sections of the Cumberland and nearby Rockcastle River are popular for whitewater canoeing, rafting, and kayaking.

The Nathan McClure Trail winds by Lake Cumberland and is well traveled by horseback riders, who often cover the full sixteen miles in a day. The path, named for a Revolutionary War hero, passes over scenic ridges and along several streams. Little Lick Campground at one end of the trail is equipped with a corral and hitching rail.

Riding is also popular in the Daniel Boone's second wilderness area, Beaver Creek, south of Lake Cumberland. Vertical sandstone cliffs create many rockhouses in the area, which sheltered both prehistoric people and early pioneers. Many streams flow through the wilderness, creating a collection of scenic waterfalls. The Sheltowee Trace does not go through the area, however. There are no maintained trails, so visitors should be adept with a compass. Just south and west of the wilderness stands another imposing geological structure, the natural arch. This sandstone

bridge stands fifty feet tall and ninety feet long and is the centerpiece of a 945-acre recreation area laced with trails.

The second part of the forest, the Redbird Ranger District, is located to the east along the Daniel Boone Parkway. The parkway cuts through the middle of the ranger district, east to west, while the Redbird River bisects the area north to south. The sixty-four-mile Redbird Crest Trail explores part of the forest, including a scenic wildlife management area intersected by a network of creeks. Big Double Creek Picnic Area provides access to the loop trail and is a popular spot for fishing. The Redbird Fitness National Recreation Trail is three-tenths of a mile long and is located near the ranger station south of the town of Big Creek. Cawood Recreation Area is the only developed campground in the district and is south of Helton on U.S. Highway 421.

About twenty miles farther south is Cumberland Gap National Historical Park, which commemorates the breech in the Appalachian Mountains where Daniel Boone and other pioneers forged their way into this land Boone called Eden. ♣

Heavy mist seen from Auxier Ridge shrouds the Red River Gorge, noted for rock shelters and arches. ADAM JONES

Daniel Boone
NATIONAL FOREST DIRECTORY

POINTS OF INTEREST

Morehead District Office and Visitor Center Information about the forest and interpretive displays are part of a new center near Cave Run Lake. Located off Highway 801, Morehead, KY 40351 (606) 784-6428

Gladie Historic Site and Information Station Forest details and interpretive activities presented in a restored log cabin in the Red River Gorge Geological Area. Open 10 a.m. to 6 p.m. daily from Memorial Day weekend through Labor Day weekend. Located on State Hwy. 715.

Natural Arch Scenic Area 945 acres with a giant sandstone bridge, trails, and picnic ground. Take U. S. 27 south from Somerset for twenty-one miles. Turn west on KY 927 for two miles.

WILDERNESS AREAS

Clifty Wilderness 13,300 acres in the Red River Gorge Geological Area. Rugged terrain with cliffs, canyons, arches, and creeks.

Beaver Creek Wilderness 4,791 acres below the clifflines of the Beaver Creek drainage. Streams, waterfalls, hardwoods, and sandstone cliffs.

RECREATIONAL OPPORTUNITIES

Hiking and Riding More than 460 miles of hiking trails, including the Sheltowee Trace and Red River Gorge National Recreational Trails. Horseback riding is permitted on many trail sections. Ask for maps from ranger offices.

Camping Twenty-five campgrounds throughout the forest, including boat-in areas on Cave Run and Laurel River Lakes. Dispersed camping is allowed in most areas. Campgrounds generally open in late April and close in November. Concessionaires operate Zilpo Campground on Cave Run Lake, and Grove and Holly Bay campgrounds on Laurel River Lake. Reservations accepted; call (800)-283-2267.

Scenic Drives Zilpo Scenic Byway is a 9.1-mile route through the northern part of the forest. Scenic vistas overlook Cave Run Lake. The byway passes through the Pioneer Weapons Area and is colorful in summer with rhododendron and mountain laurel blossoms.

Canoeing, Kayaking and Rafting Sections of the Red, Rockcastle, and Cumberland Rivers have whitewater and calmer stretches popular for floating. Outfitters rent equipment.

Hunting Deer, turkey, ruffed grouse, squirrel, and other game. Kentucky regulations apply and state license is required.

Fishing Excellent muskie fishing in Cave Run Lake, as well as largemouth bass, bluegill, crappie, and catfish. Laurel River Lake has similar fish and good rainbow trout populations. Lake Cumberland is also a popular fishing spot. More than fifty-six miles of streams are stocked in the forest. Kentucky regulations apply and state license is required.

Cross-Country Skiing All hiking trails are open for skiing and many forest roads. Tunnel Ridge Road or Forest Road 39 in the Red River Gorge Geological Area is especially popular, as well as the Twin Knobs Recreation Area at Cave Run Lake.

Off-Highway Vehicles Sections of trails are open to off-road vehicles. Get maps from ranger stations.

Mountain Bicycling All roads and most trails except those in Wilderness and Red River Gorge Geologic Area are open.

Shooting Free target practice at Clear Creek (Morehead Ranger District), Whitman Branch (London Ranger District), and Appletree (Stearns Ranger District). Open year round, sunrise to sunset.

ADMINISTRATIVE OFFICES

Forest Headquarters 100 Vaught Road, Winchester, KY 40391 (606) 745-3100

Morehead Ranger District P. O. Box 910, Morehead, KY 40351 (606) 784-6428

Stanton Ranger District 705 W. College Ave., Stanton, KY 40380 (606) 663-2852

Berea Ranger District 1835 Big Hill Road, Berea, KY 40403 (606) 986-8434

London Ranger District P. O. Box 907, U. S. Hwy. 25 South, London, KY 40743 (606) 864-4163

Somerset Ranger District 156 Realty Lane, Somerset, KY 42501 (606) 679-2018

Stearns Ranger District P. O. Box 429, U. S. Hwy. 27 North, Whitley City, KY 42653 (606) 376-5323

Redbird Ranger District HC 68, Box 65, Big Creek, KY 40914 (606) 598-2192

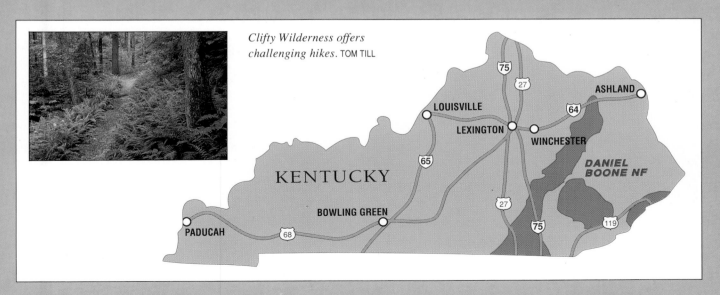

Clifty Wilderness offers challenging hikes. TOM TILL

KENTUCKY

PADUCAH
BOWLING GREEN
LOUISVILLE
LEXINGTON
WINCHESTER
ASHLAND
DANIEL BOONE NF

The Cherokee National Forest in eastern Tennessee has many soaring peaks, typical of the Appalachian Mountains. Flame azaleas, which can range in color from pale yellow to deep scarlet, prefer these lofty habitats. The deciduous shrubs often produce blossoms and leaves simultaneously, starting in May. LARRY ULRICH

Cherokee

Appalachian playground

Although no lumberjacks are likely to rouse nearby before dawn, overnight visitors at Double Camp Recreation Area do sleep on the grounds of an old lumber camp. Loggers lived in this temporary community in 1928, one of several converted to campgrounds in Tennessee's only national forest, the Cherokee.

Stretching 630,000 acres along the state's eastern border from Chattanooga to Bristol, the Cherokee is steeped in colorful history and rich in the grandeur of the Appalachian Mountains. The forest is separated into two sections by Great Smoky Mountains National Park and shares other boundaries with national forests in Georgia, North Carolina, and Virginia. The result is a magnificent, enormous tapestry of public lands well-traveled by an appreciative population. Eight million people each year visit the Cherokee.

The scenery is what appeals to many, particularly the dozens of mountain peaks, many of them soaring well above 5,000 feet. Even in geological measure, the Appalachians are ancient, dating to 500 million years ago when they were uplifted by the collision of the continental plates. Some think that the range was once higher than the Rocky Mountains and the Alps, and that weather and erosion wore them down to present heights. Geologists see two parts to this span of the

Appalachians—the Blue Ridge Province, and the Ridge and Valley Province. The Great Smoky Mountains fall within the 550 miles of the Blue Ridge Province, while the limestone ridges dotted with caves and springs interspersed among valleys constitute the second province.

The alternating contours dictate a fascinating assortment of life forms in the Cherokee, including twenty-one endangered species. Hardwoods, pines, and spruce-fir trees all grow in a complex mosaic of ecosystems hospitable to wildlife and vegetation typical of land both farther north and south. There are also intriguing grassy balds, the origins of which confound scientists. Seven whitewater rivers, all being considered for wild and scenic status, further contribute to the landscape's variety—and to recreational possibilities. Floating the rivers is widely popular. Also well-used are 660 miles of trails that allow close observation of the forest, home to more than 120 bird species and forty-seven species of mammals. Among them is the fearsome and elusive wild Russian boar. The first boar escaped from a hunting preserve in 1912, and their sharp-tusked and aggressive progeny are favored game for hunters.

Varied, too, is the chain of human life in the forest, beginning more than 10,000 years ago with prehistoric Indians. Other prehistoric residents built ceremonial mounds about a thousand years ago characteristic of a highly developed culture spread across the South. But these people, at least the early ones, some anthropologists think, were not the ancestors of the Cherokee Indians, for whom the forest is named. The first white Euro-American occupants were mostly lone hunters and traders, followed by families who raised sheep, pigs, and cattle, and farmed the rugged mountains as best they could.

It was the farmers, some believe, who caused the grassy balds to develop. Grazing herds in the high country in warmer months was common practice for years, and theorists propose that this prevented the usual succession of plant species to trees. Others, however, note that some balds existed before farmers arrived. They

Roan Mountain looms snowy white over a fertile green valley and extends from Tennessee to North Carolina. JEFF HYDER

contend that balds resulted from repeated forest fires. Or perhaps buffalo, which possibly existed in the area centuries ago, overgrazed the balds. Eighty-some grassy balds are found in the long Appalachian range coursing through the eastern United States, and whatever their origin, they offer unmatched vistas and habitat for a fascinating array of species.

Extensive logging occurred in this part of Tennessee as it did through much of the East, with entire mountainsides laid bare within a short time. Until the trees were gone, jobs were plentiful, and lumber companies built makeshift settlements like Double Camp, sometimes housing loggers and their families in railroad boxcars. Loggers worked ten hours a day, six days a week for wages of about twenty cents per hour.

The federal government acquired and restored the lands in the Cherokee beginning in 1911, with the present-day forest officially established in 1936. Great Smoky Mountains National Park opened in 1940, partly intended as a magnet for a new tourist industry, which has steadily grown.

While the Cherokee is once again a productive timber source, with about thirty million board feet harvested in a year, the forest also plays an important part in providing recreation for the millions of visitors attracted by the region's reputation. Besides hiking trails, including portions of the famed Appalachian Trail, there are 108 miles of horse trails and sixty-one miles of trails for

all-terrain vehicles and motorcycles. Lakes, ponds, and 750 miles of streams are found throughout the forest, many of them prime fishing waters. The Cherokee also boasts the first national forest scenic byway in the country, designated in 1988. Located in the southern section of the forest between Cleveland on the west and Ducktown on the east, the Ocoee Scenic Byway is made up of U.S. Highway 64 and Forest Service Road 77. The twenty-six-mile route passes through a representative spectrum of the Cherokee's

Above right: While no river otters may be seen on the Cherokee at this time, plans are in the works to reintroduce these playful mammals to the Nolichucky and Hiwassee rivers in 1993-94. GARRY WALTER

Right: Canoeing the rollicking Hiwassee River is immensely popular, especially in summer. PHOTO COURTESY OF USDA FOREST SERVICE

most renowned features, starting on the west of the forest where Big Frog, Chilhowee, and Sugarloaf mountains first come into view. Sugarloaf's conical shape looms over Parksville Lake, formed by the damming of the Ocoee River, which races through a rugged rock gorge where the byway also travels. The 1,950-acre lake, also called Ocoee Lake, is popular for water sports and lakeshore camping, and at 838 feet occupies the lowest elevation on the drive.

Near the lake, Forest Service Road 77 becomes a spur of the scenic byway as it climbs Chilhowee Mountain, the drive's highest point at 2,200 feet. The mountain itself reaches to 2,600 feet; fall colors here are especially vivid, with red, scarlet, and chestnut oaks, dogwoods, maples, black locusts and sourwoods mixed with shortleaf, white, and Virginia pines. There

are several pull-offs on the steady climb, with good views of the wide Tennessee Valley, as well as Parksville Lake and other mountains many miles away. There is a short loop trail at the Parksville Lake Overlook and picnic tables at the Sugarloaf Overlook. Another era of the region's history, the Civil War, is described in an interpretive sign at "Confederate Camp" along Forest Service Road 77. Although Tennessee was a major battleground for the Confederacy, a majority of mountain residents voted against secession, possibly because few owned the wealth of slaves claimed by lowland planters.

Chilhowee Recreation Area on the mountaintop offers camping, swimming, and fishing in a seven-acre lake, and trails for bicycling and hiking. The half-mile Chilhowee Forest Walk explores the area around

RETURNING

Everyone enjoys recognition for hard work, and Forest Service employees are no exception. The stewards of the Cherokee National Forest are justifiably proud of their top award among southern national forests for outstanding fisheries management.

Both sport fish like brook trout and endangered species such as the Smoky madtom, a catfish known to exist only in the forest, benefit from restoration efforts. Forest managers, cooperating with wildlife specialists from other agencies, are replacing introduced species like rainbow and brown trout in scattered streams with native brook trout, which have declined significantly because of pressures from the introduced fish. For the endangered catfish, they are removing eggs so the young can be safely raised, and then returned to the wild.

Efforts are also underway to encourage bald eagles to nest in

the forest again. Although migrating eagles are seen, nesting birds are extremely rare—just one pair of eagles has nested in the Cherokee in past years. Thirty young eaglets are being released in stages over three years near South Holston Lake, after first spending time in hacking towers twenty feet off the

ground. The eaglets are fed until they are old enough to fly, then released. Typically, mated pairs return to nest near sites where one of them learned to fly.

A tree placed across Horse Creek creates a pool for trout. PHOTO COURTESY OF USDA FOREST SERVICE

McKamy Lake, while another path leads to Benton Falls, one of many scenic waterfalls in the forest. A delicate wild orchid—the pink lady slipper—may be visible along these and other trails, as well as dozens of other wildflower varieties. Chances for seeing wildlife are also good because the Forest Service has deliberately cleared several areas to attract animals along the Arbutus Watchable Wildlife Trail in the Chilhowee Recreation Area. Songbirds, as well as deer, turkeys, and squirrels are drawn to the plant foods that grow after ground is cleared.

As the byway continues back on U.S. Highway 64, rafters and kayakers can be seen challenging the swift waters of the Ocoee River, rated among the top ten whitewater streams in the country. Outfitters provide equipment and guides from March until November, but summer brings the most floaters. Beyond forest boundaries, the highway reaches Copperhill and Ducktown, where copper ore smelting beginning in the 1800s caused so much pollution that much of the terrain remained eerily barren years later. Ducktown Copper Basin Museum explains the industry and has buildings and equipment from early copper mining.

North of the Ocoee is the Hiwassee River, also noted for rapids, flowing in a winding path across the width of the Cherokee. Designated as a state scenic river, the Hiwassee is also popular for floating and there are two campgrounds nearby. The John Muir

Above right: Endangered bald eagles are being reintroduced to the Cherokee.
TOM STACK & ASSOCIATES
Right: Scenic drives draw thousands of visitors annually.
PHOTO COURTESY OF USDA FOREST SERVICE

National Recreation Trail follows many of the river's bends, retracing for nineteen miles the steps of the writer and naturalist born in 1838 who walked from Georgia to Kentucky.

East of Indian Boundary Recreation Area, (IBRA), site of an 1819 treaty boundary corner between the Cherokee Nation and United States, black bears are sometimes spotted feeding on berries along Tennessee Highway 165. At the recreation area, the ninety-six-acre lake attracts many birds and other wildlife. The four-mile IBRA hiking and bicycling trail is a newly designated "Watchable Wildlife" trail with enhancements to attract birds, fish, and a variety of other animals.

The northern reaches of the Cherokee above the national park feature over 250 miles of hiking trails, including long stretches of the Appalachian Trail, which weaves in and out of Tennessee and North Carolina forests. Among many spectacular sights along the path are the Roan Mountain peaks, where spruce-fir forests, grassy balds, and heath balds covered in Catawba rhododendron, mountain laurel, and high-bush blueberries are found. At Carver's Gap, off Tennessee Highway 143 on the state line between Tennessee and North Carolina, rises the longest stretch of grassy balds in the world. Peregrine falcons, osprey, and bald and golden eagles are among the raptors seen migrating over the gap in fall, while in winter, snow buntings are occasional visitors to the balds. Rhododendron blossoms attract ruby-throated hummingbirds in June.

Year-round, the spruce-fir forests draw northern saw-whet owls, pine siskins, common ravens, and red-winged crossbills.

The Unaka Mountain Auto Tour is a thirty-mile loop that features similar terrain, including the aptly-titled Beauty Spot Gap with its profusion of wildflowers. An old silver mine nearby, along with eleven other stops on the route, are described in a brochure available at the Unaka District Ranger's Office. Be on the lookout for deer, rabbits, foxes, and ruffed grouse, just a few of the animals that forage in the balds.

Trout fishing is one of the Cherokee's best-known attractions, and there are both stocked and wild streams. Rainbow, brown, and brook trout are all found in the forest, with concerted efforts underway to encourage proliferation of native brook trout (see sidebar story). The Nolichucky and French Broad are the whitewater rivers flowing through the northern half of the forest, both served by commercial outfitters. Two large lakes offer other recreational possibilities. Watauga Lake and South Holston Lake are separated by the Holston and Iron Mountains, and each has boat ramps and camping facilities. South Holston Lake is the site of efforts to encourage bald eagles to nest in the forest (see sidebar story).

Besides excellent fishing waters, some of the forest's streams are also favorite places for recreational gold panning. In fact, people have searched for gold in the Tennessee mountains since the days of Spanish explorer Hernando de Soto in the 1500s. De Soto failed in his quest, and few today are likely to strike it rich on the stray bits of gold that surface here and there. Still, the prospect of chancing onto a good-sized nugget keeps some optimists busy sifting through water for hours. No permit is required as long as streams are not significantly disturbed. Even without finding gold, many enjoy the interesting pebbles and stones that surface in their pans. As long as panning is pursued for personal—not commercial—gain, visitors are welcome to keep any gold they might find. ♣

The Bald River, over eons, carved out scenic stretches in the Bald River Gorge Wilderness. The Cherokee has eleven wilderness areas. LAURENCE PARENT

Cherokee
NATIONAL FOREST DIRECTORY

POINTS OF INTEREST

Roan Mountain Largest stretch of unusual grassy balds in the world and colorful rhododendron-covered heaths and spruce-fir forests. The annual Rhododendron Festival in June draws thousands. Take U. S. 321 south from Elizabethton to Hampton; turn right on U. S. 19 E for ten miles to the town of Roan Mountain. Turn right on Tennessee 143 for twelve miles.

Bald River Falls Often photographed cascade. Take Tennessee Scenic Route 165 east from Tellico Plains; continue on 165 east at fork in road outside Tellico Plains; turn right at signs to Bald River Falls on Forest Service Road 210 for seven miles.

Chilhowee Recreation Area Mountaintop facilities in a scenic setting. Take U. S. 64 east from Cleveland for twelve miles; turn left on Forest Service Road 77 for seven miles.

Tellico-Robinsville Road (Tennessee Scenic Route 165) very scenic, with excellent views of the area.

WILDERNESS AREAS

Joyce Kilmer-Slickrock 3,832 acres; this wilderness overlaps with 6,400 acres in bordering North Carolina.

Gee Creek 2,493 acres.

Cohutta 1,795 acres; 35,247 more acres of the Cohutta lie in Georgia.

Big Frog 7,986 acres.

Citico Creek 16,226 acres adjoining Joyce Kilmer-Slickrock Wilderness.

Bald River Gorge 3,721 acres.

Little Frog Mountain 4,684 acres.

Pond Mountain 6,665 acres.

Unaka Mountain 4,700 acres.

Big Laurel Branch 6,251 acres.

Sampson Mountain 7,992 acres.

RECREATIONAL OPPORTUNITIES

Hiking and Riding More than 660 miles of trails, including 180 miles of the Appalachian Trail, which meanders from Georgia to Maine. More than fifty-six miles of horse trails located throughout the forest.

Camping Thirty campgrounds across the forest. Most close in winter. Dispersed camping is permitted, with some restrictions. Check with the ranger station for current guidelines.

Scenic Drives Ocoee Scenic Byway, in the southern half of the forest, passes through Ocoee River Gorge, by Parksville Lake, and up a mountain with panoramic views. Take U. S. Highway 64 heading east from Cleveland. The twenty-six-mile route has a spur up Forest Service Road 77 to mountaintop Chilhowee Recreation Area. The Unaka Mountain Auto Tour is a thirty-mile loop in the Unaka Ranger District in the northern half of the forest. Brochure available about twelve stops along the way, including a grassy bald and abandoned silver mine.

Information about other scenic drives available at each district ranger's office.

Kayaking and Rafting Seven whitewater rivers flow through the forest. The Ocoee and Hiwassee are most popular for floating. Outfitters provide equipment and guides from March through November.

Hunting Russian wild boar attract nationwide attention. Deer, turkey, squirrel, ruffed grouse, and other game. License required from Tennessee Wildlife Resources Agency.

Fishing Lakes, ponds, and 750 miles of streams are suitable for fishing. Rainbow, brown, and brook trout are favored, while smallmouth bass and bream are plentiful.

Cross-Country Skiing Only highest elevations in the northern part of the forest are ski-worthy and these only sporadically, depending on widely variable snowfall.

Off-Road Vehicles Sixty-one miles of trails for all-terrain vehicles and motorcycles are located throughout the forest. Maps available from ranger stations.

ADMINISTRATIVE OFFICES

Forest Headquarters 2800 North Ocoee Street, P.O. Box 2010, Cleveland, TN 37320, (615) 476-9700

Ocoee Ranger District Route 1, Box 348 D, Benton, TN 37307, (615) 338-5201

Hiwassee Ranger District Route 1, Mecca Pike, Drawer D, Etowah, TN 37331, (615) 263-5486

Tellico Ranger District Route 3, P.O. Box 339, Tellico River Road, Tellico Plains, TN 37385, (615) 253-2520

Nolichucky Ranger District 120 Austin Avenue, Greeneville, TN 37743, (615) 638-4109

Unaka Ranger District 1205 N. Main Street, Erwin, TN 37650, (615) 743-4452

Watauga Ranger District Route 9, Box 2235, Elizabethton, TN 37643, (615) 542-2942

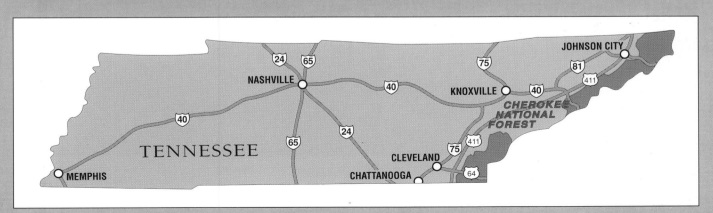

Little Santeetlah Creek, hidden within the Nantahalah National Forest in western North Carolina, flows through the Joyce Kilmer Memorial Forest and Slickrock Wilderness. Kilmer was a soldier and poet who wrote the famous lines, "I think that I shall never see a poem lovely as a tree." LAURENCE PARENT

North Carolina

Pisgah • Nantahala • Uwharrie • Croatan

N A T I O N A L F O R E S T S

Mountains to the sea

Mountains climbing into the clouds, gold mine shafts burrowing into the earth, salty wetlands reaching towards the sea—all of these are found in North Carolina's four national forests. Totaling more than one million acres, they are among the nation's most visited, offering 1,700 miles of trails, 800 campsites, eleven wilderness areas, and hundreds of streams in a collection of lands from the Appalachian Mountains to the Atlantic Coast.

Apart from tourism, the forests produce some fifty-six million board feet of timber annually, much of it valuable hardwoods for the state's renowned furniture makers. At the same time, forest managers are at the forefront in efforts to restore ecosystems, repairing 149 acres of eroded land in a year, and planting seedlings or assisting in natural regeneration of trees on 5,700 acres. Such preparations for future needs follow a long tradition in North Carolina, where the science of American forestry began on ground now included in the national forests.

Pisgah

A photograph could never fully capture the shock of color blanketing Roan Mountain when catawba rhododendrons bloom in summer. The bushes extend too far on this and other surrounding grassy balds, and it's doubtful that film could reproduce the flowers' intense purple hue. Perhaps that explains why thousands come to see the display for themselves. Even the elderly with canes climb the steep Appalachian Trail spanning the mountain in the Pisgah National Forest in northwestern North Carolina.

Past the first wave of rhododendrons grow meadows where cool breezes whip through knee-high grasses, making them ripple like Kansas wheat. The browns and greens of these mountain oatgrasses and sedges form muted backdrops for more rhododendrons. In other places, nodding yellow wildflowers mingle with coppery petals of flame azaleas. Ahead, and at every point on the horizon, stand more mountains reaching toward the sky.

The Pisgah, covering a half-million acres, has many breathtaking peaks, including Mount Mitchell, highest point east of the Mississippi River at 6,684 feet. Vegetation usually found much farther north, such as Fraser fir, grows on some of these pinnacles, remnants of the retreating ice age. Mount Mitchell is among the most popular forest attractions, with Mount Mitchell State Park on the mountaintop. Even a difficult trail to the summit is well traveled, with hikers often starting

THE CRADLE OF FORESTRY IN AMERICA

The Cradle of Forestry, while a museum of sorts, is not at all stuffy. Touching—even smelling—exhibits is encouraged, especially in the outdoor section. A guide may invite a tour member on one of two historic interpre-

tive trails to sniff the spicy sassafras tree, source of root beer flavoring, or to feel the hewn timbers of one of the original buildings from the nation's first forestry school. Several historic buildings, patterned after Germany's Black Forest lodges, are open and authentically furnished from the late 1800s in this special attraction in the Pisgah National Forest. An old portable sawmill and logging train are also displayed.

Inside the spacious visitor center, more interactive exhibits explain how American forestry

Tour guides explain both the buildings and vegetation.
SHARYN KANE/RICHARD KEETON

developed and introduce two individuals largely responsible—Carl Schenck and Gifford Pinchot. Both spent their early careers working for millionaire George Vanderbilt in what is now the Pisgah National Forest. Pinchot, the first American forester, helped Vanderbilt improve his forest lands. Schenck started the first forestry school in America, the Biltmore Forest School, where he shared his knowledge of trees and the environment with students. Pinchot went on to become the first chief of the Forest Service and influenced national policy for years after his passing, a fitting legacy for one appalled by the extensive forest destruction he saw early in his life.

---

from Black Mountain Campground. As the path threads upward, temperatures drop and clouds float across the red spruce and fir trees. On a clear day, the view extends seventy miles and encompasses a distressing sight among the beauty: many firs on Mount Mitchell are dead or dying. Scientists studying the problem disagree about causes. Some say balsam wooly aphids are largely responsible; others cite pollution.

Altogether, 850 miles of trails wind through the Pisgah, named for a Biblical peak from which Moses saw the Promised Land. The Black Mountain Crest Trail travels from Mount Mitchell across several of the Black Mountains, a small but wonderfully high range

Left: *Thousands make the annual summer pilgrimage to see the flowering of the catawba rhododendrons on Roan Mountain in the Pisgah National Forest.* TAD STAMM
Right: *Sliding Rock provides a free thrill for participants and onlookers.* KEVIN ADAMS

with six of the ten tallest crests in the East. The trail—exceptionally scenic but also quite rugged, like all of the trails in this area—intersects with Colbert Ridge Trail, which descends to Carolina Hemlocks Campground. Swimming, tubing, and fishing in the South Toe River are popular pastimes here. Float trips are also common on several Pisgah rivers, especially the Nolichucky and French Broad. Also skirting the upper reaches of Mount Mitchell is the Buncombe Horse Trail, one of several in the forest. Camping permits are required.

Linville Gorge Wilderness, east of Mount Mitchell, is laced with trails where hikers can take in the sights below the horizon. Steep descents travel through dark thickets of mountain laurel, a trip that can be disorienting. Hikers sometimes become lost, which usually could be avoided by a stop first for recommendations at the visitor's center near the gorge. Despite such caveats, hiking Linville Gorge is a wonderful excursion, with a fine view of Linville River at the bottom. Unusual rock formations also attract rock climbers. But the chasm can be enjoyed from above, too, by the more casual visitor from an overlook at Wiseman's View on Kistler Memorial Highway. "Highway" is a misnomer for this dirt road, but a fine panorama of the gorge makes the drive worthwhile. Paved trails—one of them accessible to the disabled—lead to an observation point.

Perhaps the Pisgah's most preferred drive is south of Asheville along the Forest Heritage Scenic Byway, which passes many forest highlights, including the Cradle of Forestry, a fascinating indoor/outdoor museum (see sidebar story). Also popular is Looking Glass Falls, one of many area waterfalls, and Sliding Rock, a natural water slide. The byway also skirts picnic areas, Davidson River Campground, and the Pisgah Ranger District Station and information center where there are informative exhibits and a nature trail.

Nantahala

"Wayah" is a Cherokee Indian word for "wolf," and it's easy to imagine one peering out from the mist along the curving drive up Wayah Bald in the Nantahala National Forest in southwestern North Carolina. Rain from an earlier shower drips from trees long afterwards. The road goes by the historic Wilson Lick Ranger Station, built when riding a horse and shooting straight were required for all forest employees. Finally, at the crest of Wayah Bald at 5,200 feet, there is an observation tower where the sweet scent of white azaleas hangs in the moist air. Fog obscures the view, but on drier days the mountains of both Tennessee and Georgia are visible from the place of the wolf.

The state's largest forest

Below: The vibrant colors of autumn make the mountainous Nantahala National Forest a popular scenic drive. BILL LEA

with more than one-half million acres, the Nantahala is noted for spectacular Appalachian Mountains, many surpassing heights of 4,000 feet. The high elevations extend the spring season for months, delighting wildflower enthusiasts. Trails crisscross the peaks, including the Bartram and Appalachian Trails, which merge as they climb Wayah Bald. Both cover many scenic miles, although the Bartram Trail is less known than the busy Appalachian Trail that extends eighty-eight miles through the Nantahala.

"Nantahala" is another Cherokee word meaning "land of the noonday sun," and originally applied to the Nantahala River Gorge, where sunlight doesn't reach the bottom until mid-day because of the gorge's depth and thick vegetation. Floating the white-water river is among the forest's biggest draws, beckoning some 200,000 people annually. The Nantahala is navigable for eight miles, with Class II and III rapids.

The Mountain Waters Scenic Byway provides access to the gorge and other forest highlights. The route covers sixty-one miles beginning at Highlands and ending southwest of Bryson City, following state and federal highways. Besides Nantahala River Gorge, the byway leads to Cullasaja River Gorge, Wayah Bald, the Appalachian Trail, and the town of Franklin, the "gem capitol" of the South.

Other water attractions exist throughout the forest, including streams with stocked and native trout, and scenic

Enormous tulip poplars dwarf and fascinate visitors to the Joyce Kilmer Memorial Forest.
LAURENCE PARENT

waterfalls. Whitewater Falls, east of Highlands, crashes 411 feet, while Cullasaja Falls and Dry Falls are both just west of the town. Highlands is also close to the wild and scenic Chattooga and Horsepasture Rivers and Whiteside Mountain, where a short loop trail flanks sheer cliffs. Many lakes with lyrical Indian names are also nestled in the Nantahala; Santeetlah, Hiwassee, Chatuge, Appalachia, Nantahala, and Fontana are some of the largest. Campgrounds are often overlooked in these recreation areas, which offer excellent fishing and clean—if chilly—water for swimming.

Near Lake Santeetlah is the popular Joyce Kilmer Memorial Forest, named for the man who penned the famous lines, "I think that I shall never see a poem lovely as a tree." The unusually large preserve of old-growth trees spans 3,800 acres of poplars, beeches, and hemlocks, some 300 years old. Trails wind by the giants, many of which soar so high it's impossible to

see their crowns from the ground. Some of the trees have girths as impressive as their heights. In more than one case, up to five adults are needed to reach all the way around the trunk of a tree. The area is part of the Joyce Kilmer-Slickrock Wilderness, a region of high, rocky terrain.

The Nantahala features many other spots slightly off the beaten path. South of the Joyce Kilmer-Slickrock Wilderness is the challenging Snowbird Creek Basin, reportedly the final refuge for Indians ordered to leave their homelands. The region still seems wild and remote, although hiking trails ease the way.

A legend about an Indian turned into stone surrounds Standing Indian Basin on the outskirts of the Southern Nantahala Wilderness near Georgia. The basin is honeycombed with hiking and riding trails. One leads to Laurel Falls, a gentle cascade, and another to the John Wasilik tree, the nation's second-largest poplar. Both hikes are less than a mile and start near Forest Service Road 67, which also heads to the backcountry information center and Standing Indian Campground. Searching for the rock pillar resembling an Indian is one of the Nantahala's many entertaining possibilities.

Uwharrie
N A T I O N A L   F O R E S T

Eons ago, when North American and African continents collided, a chain of islands was caught in the powerful squeeze and thrust upward. These became the Uwharrie Mountains, which were then worn away

Cow parsnip, snakeroot, and bee balm. ADAM JONES

by rivers to only about 1,000 feet above sea level. Some believe this range may be North America's oldest, and it is the Uwharrie Mountains that form the backbone of the Uwharrie National Forest in south-central North Carolina.

The Piedmont forest has long been popular with hunters stalking deer and other game. But in many ways, the Uwharrie is largely undiscovered. Only recently have campers and hikers begun to scout its 49,000 acres to any degree, but efforts are underway to encourage more visitors. New recreation facilities are being planned, primarily near Badin Lake, including a swimming beach and visitor center. Horse trails and an equestrian campground are also planned, along with more tent and recreational vehicle camping, and boat access for float trips on the Uwharrie River. Boating is already popular among local residents, as well as fishing and watching for eagles near the Narrows Dam.

Even before the improvements are added, however, there is reason to explore the forest. Hikers can travel twenty miles on the Uwharrie National Recreation Trail. The Ranger Station, near Troy, also has a pleasant nature trail on the grounds overlooking Densons Creek; brochures identifying vegetation and other features are available. Trails also pass through

PROTECTING THE PAST

Only a knowledgeable eye would recognize the hundreds of scattered rocks in the Uwharrie National Forest as a sign of pre-

historic human life, which is probably just as well. Too many already see archeological sites as places to steal. Despite federal laws against taking artifacts from government land, and fines up to $500,000, thefts are common. Vandalism is also widespread—and costly. Estimated expenses to repair damaged archeological sites in southern forests are $4 million. But money cannot replace knowledge lost to looters, whose digging

Archeologist Michael Harmon examines artifacts at a prehistoric site.
SHARYN KANE/RICHARD KEETON

for objects destroys soil layering, the crucial map to earlier life.

The scattered stones in the Uwharrie are left from prehistoric hunters who made rock spear points and other tools. Marks they made on the stones remain thousands of years later and tell scientists much about the hunters' habits—but only if no one takes or destroys the artifacts. The Forest Service asks visitors to help preserve archeological sites by leaving them undisturbed and by reporting any violations.

Birkhead Mountain Wilderness, which offers backcountry recreation.

Abandoned mines exist in several areas of the Uwharrie. Few outside the region know that the first gold rush in the nation occurred near the forest in 1799. Within the forest, the Russell Mine was among the biggest operations in the late 1800s and among its remaining vestiges is Big Cut, a hole sixty feet deep. At the bottom, dark shafts extend even farther. Not far away lie the ruins of a stamp factory where rock was crushed, then mixed with chemicals to leach out precious ore.

An interesting geological area, locally called Nifty Rocks, can be found near Badin Lake. Enormous boulders, some fifteen feet tall, are arranged almost like walled rooms with passageways. Climb to the top of one and the glittering waters of Badin Lake are visible below.

Hunting is popular on the Uwharrie, and quail are one of the favored game birds. BILL LEA

Croatan

The male fiddler crab engages in an interesting ritual to attract a mate. He waves his fiddle-shaped claw, and curious females, who don't have such appendages, respond. Hundreds of the tiny crustaceans can be spotted when the salty waters recede along the Cedar Point Tideland Trail in the Croatan National Forest. Located on the coast of the Atlantic Ocean, the Croatan is an ideal place to observe such species unusual in a southern national forest. Here, for instance, is one of the few habitats for the unusual Venus fly trap, a deceptively small plant that captures insects in its lima-bean-shaped clutches, then devours them to compensate for mineral deficiencies in soils. The plant is one of five insectivorous species in the forest, which covers 157,000 acres.

The Croatan's name again derives from an Indian language, in this case from the Algonquin word for "council town." Another Indian word common in forest descriptions is "pocosin," meaning "swamp on a hill." Pocosins are poorly drained ground underlaid by deposits of organic, highly acidic muck, sometimes six feet deep. The conditions stunt vegetation growth, with trees reaching only five-foot heights. Near the edge of a pocosin, however, the muck thins to several inches and pond pines grow robustly, up to sixty feet tall. The understory also flourishes with titi and other species sprawling together in a nearly impenetrable thicket.

Water is abundant in many forms, with 4,300 acres of lakes, popular for boating and canoeing, and sections of the Neuse and White Oak Rivers, made salty by mingling with the ocean. The mixing of salt and fresh water, forming brackish water, allows the Croatan to harbor salt water estuaries where so much of ocean life begins. Salt water anglers gather near the lower reaches of the Neuse River near Pine Cliff Recreation Area, site of a wide sandy beach also popular with hikers and picnickers. There is also another sand beach near Neuse River Campground.

Hikers can choose from the easy Cedar Point Tideland Trail and Island Creek Forest Walk to the more difficult Neusiok Trail. Two observation blinds along the tideland path are popular for watching herons and other birds common in the forest, which is on the migratory Atlantic flyway. Interpretive signs dot the path, much of which is comprised of boardwalks over tidal marshes. The Island Creek Forest Walk offers a scenic stroll along the clear creek and through a mature hardwood forest.

Wildlife is abundant along the Neusiok Trail, lacing for twenty miles through pocosins, hardwood sections, and pine flatlands before ending at the Newport River. Often wet and muddy, the trail is avoided in summer because of heat, insects, and poisonous snakes. But in cooler weather, the hike is an enjoyable challenge, with a chance to see alligators, bears, bobcats, and foxes. ♣

Below: Male fiddler crabs in the Croatan attract females by waving their appendages. SUSAN M. GLASCOCK
Above right: Snow geese fill the sky over the coastal waters in the Croatan. BILL LEA

Pisgah
NATIONAL FOREST DIRECTORY

Roan Mountain A high grassy bald with awe-inspiring arrays of rhododendrons. The mountain has other wildflowers and scenic views and can be reached by driving north about thirteen miles from Bakersville, North Carolina on NC 261.

Black Mountain Recreation Area Campground located at the base of a popular trail ascending Mount Mitchell, highest peak in the East. Drive to N.C. 80 south from near Burnsville for twelve miles. Turn south on Forest Service Road 472 for three miles.

Cradle of Forestry Indoor and outdoor museum dedicated to the birthplace of forestry in America. On U.S. 276, fifteen miles north of Brevard. Also can be reached from the Blue Ridge Parkway by traveling south on U.S. 276 for four miles.

WILDERNESS AREAS

Linville Gorge 10,975 acres in eastern part of the forest. A deep, lush gorge with strenuous trails. Weekend and holiday campers must obtain free Forest Service permit at ranger station in Marion, North Carolina. Hiking is extremely difficult. Wiseman's View along N. C. State Hwy. 105 offers a good view of the gorge.

Shining Rock 18,500 acres southwest of Asheville, North Carolina. A series of high-elevation ridges rib this area with the elevation reaching 6,030 feet on Cold Mountain.

Middle Prong 7,900 acres west of and adjacent to Shining Rock Wilderness. This also is a high-elevation wilderness, characterized by fir, spruce, hemlock, and hardwood forests and grassy balds.

RECREATION OPPORTUNITIES

Hiking and Riding More than 850 miles of trails including 136 miles of the Appalachian Trail. The 18.4-mile Buncombe Trail and various other paths designated for horseback riding.

Scenic Drives Forest Heritage Scenic Byway is a seventy-nine-mile loop south of Asheville that passes many sites, including Cradle of Forestry, Looking Glass Falls, and Sliding Rock. Byway's major entrance is near Brevard, North Carolina, and travels along U. S. Highway 276, N. C. Route 215, and U. S. Highway 64.

Rafting, Kayaking, and Canoeing French Broad and Nolichucky Rivers offer excellent float trip possibilities with outfitters available.

Camping and Picnicking Many opportunities. Some campgrounds accept reservations through 1-800-283-CAMP. Dispersed camping allowed in most of the forest.

Hunting Deer, turkey, bear, and other game. State regulations and licenses apply.

Fishing Upper section of Davidson River rated among top 100 trout streams in the country. Many other ideal locations for brown and rainbow trout and other fish. Some areas feature native brook trout. State regulations apply. Some areas have special requirements such as streams where fish must be caught with artificial flies and then released.

Cross-Country Skiing Popular on Roan Mountain.

Rock Climbing Looking Glass Rock offers excellent climbing with 78 routes, many rated extremely difficult. Table Rock, Hawksbill, and Sitting

Bear in Linville Gorge Wilderness in the Grandfather Ranger District have hiking routes ranging from easy to extremely difficult.

Off-Road Vehicles Brown Mountain ORV Area open to motorcycles, ATV's, and other ORVs. Contact Grandfather Ranger District. Mountain biking allowed on forest roads and designated trails.

ADMINISTRATIVE OFFICES

Forest Headquarters 100 Otis Street, Box 2750, Asheville, NC 28802 (704) 257-4200

Pisgah Ranger District 1001 Pisgah Hwy., Pisgah Forest, NC 28768 (704) 877-3265

Grandfather Ranger District P.O. Box 519, Marion, NC 28752 (704) 652-2144

Toecane Ranger District P.O. Box 128, Burnsville, NC 28714 (704) 682-6146 (On U.S. 19 By-pass in Burnsville)

French Broad Ranger District P.O. Box 128, Hot Springs, NC 28743 (704) 622-3202

Nantahala
NATIONAL FOREST DIRECTORY

POINTS OF INTEREST

Joyce Kilmer Memorial Forest 3,800 acres of old-growth trees. Part of Joyce Kilmer-Slickrock Wilderness. The two-mile Joyce Kilmer Recreation Trail loops through the forest.

Wayah Bald Mountain known for its view and fragrant white azaleas in early summer. On Forest Road 69, a gravel road, about fifteen miles west of Franklin, on NC 1310.

Wasilik Poplar Second-largest yellow poplar tree in the nation growing at the end of an easily hiked trail less than a mile long. A parking area is on Forest Road 67, two miles north of Standing Indian Campground and southwest of Franklin.

Whiteside Mountain Granite-face mountain with steep cliffs and a national recreation trail to the top. Drive northeast from Highlands on U.S. Highway 64.

WILDERNESS AREAS

Joyce Kilmer-Slickrock 17,013 acres in northwestern part of forest. Old-growth trees and high-altitude trails.

Southern Nantahala 10,900 acres in North Carolina with more territory in Georgia. Highest point is Standing Indian Mountain at 5,499 feet. Appalachian Trail meanders through the area.

Ellicott Rock 3,900 acres in North Carolina with acreage also in Georgia and South Carolina. Steep terrain and the Chattooga River.

RECREATIONAL OPPORTUNITIES

Hiking and Riding The more than 500,000 acres of the Nantahala is crisscrossed with hiking trails. Horseback riding allowed on Big Indian Loop Trail in Standing Indian Basin, Tsali Trail near Fontana Lake, and other pathways.

Camping and Picnicking Nantahala offers numerous grounds set aside for both activities. Some of the best campgrounds are near the large lakes which dot the forest. Dispersed camping allowed throughout most of the forest.

Scenic Drives State Road 1310 west of Franklin is pretty any time of year but especially in June when flame azaleas bloom.

Rafting, Kayaking, and Canoeing Nantahala River along U. S. Highway 19 is very popular.

Hunting Wild boar, deer, bear, turkey, and other game. State regulations and licenses apply.

Fishing The lakes and numerous trout streams provide excellent fishing. State regulations and licenses apply.

Off-Road Vehicles Four-wheel-drive and all-terrain vehicles, motorcycles, and mountain bikes allowed on many designated trails in Upper Tellico ORV Area near Tennessee border, north of Murphy, N.C.

ADMINISTRATIVE OFFICES

Forest Headquarters 100 Otis Street, Box 2750, Asheville, NC 28802 (704) 257-4200

Cheoah Ranger District U.S. Forest Service Route 1, Box 16-A, Robbinsville, NC 28771 (On U.S. 129 north of Robbinsville) (704) 479-6431

Highlands Ranger District Rt. 2, Box 247, Highlands, NC 28741 (704) 526-3765

Tusquitee Ranger District 201 Woodland Drive, Murphy, NC 28906 (On U.S. 19 south of Murphy) (704) 837-5152

Wayah Ranger District 8 Sloan Road, Franklin, NC 28734 (On U.S. 64 west of Franklin) (704) 524-6441

Uwharrie
NATIONAL FOREST DIRECTORY

POINTS OF INTEREST

Badin Lake Recreation Area Campground on east side of the forest.

Russell Mine Remnants of late 1800s commercial gold prospecting. Located about 2.5 miles north of Eldorado, the mining operations are near State Route 1302. Contact ranger district for details.

Nifty Rocks Unusual boulders that are fun to climb. Near Forest Service Road 576 and Lake Badin.

WILDERNESS AREAS

Birkhead 4,790 acres north of the rest of the Uwharrie Forest. Moderately steep terrain, rock outcrops, and several small streams.

RECREATIONAL OPPORTUNITIES

Hiking Best hiking is along the more than twenty-mile Uwharrie Trail. Denson's Creek Trail behind the Ranger Station near Troy is an easy nature trail.

Camping and Picnicking Badin Lake Recreation Area is the main

Hikers and climbers enjoy Looking Glass Rock. BILL LEA

campground. A group camp is nearby; reservations required through Ranger Station. Dispersed camping allowed throughout most of the forest.

Scenic Drives Forest Service Road 576 offers views of the Pee Dee River and eagles in winter. Road crosses much of the forest.

ADMINISTRATIVE OFFICES

Forest Headquarters 100 Otis St., Box 2750, Asheville, NC 28802 (704) 257-4200

Uwharrie Ranger Station Rt. 3, Box 470, Troy, NC 27371 (2 miles east of Troy on NC 27) (919) 576-6391

Croatan
NATIONAL FOREST DIRECTORY

POINTS OF INTEREST

Cedar Point Recreation Area Located near the mouth of the White Oak River, three miles east of Swansboro off NC 58, offers camping, hiking on the Cedar Point Tideland Trail, picnicking, fishing, and canoeing.

Neusiok Trail A wild, twenty-mile walkway requiring hikers to wear boots for sloshing through swampy areas. Begin at either Newport River or Pinecliff Recreation Area on the Neuse River, about ten miles from intersection of U. S. Highway 70 and State Highway 10. Picnicking is popular at Pinecliff, as well as fishing in the river.

Neuse River Recreation Area Located in an area known as Flanners Beach on the Neuse River, ten miles south of New Bern, along U.S. Highway 70. Camping, swimming, and picnicking available.

WILDERNESS AREAS

Four wilderness areas include **Catfish Lake South** 7,600 acres; **Pocosin**, 11,000 acres; **Pond Pine**, 1,860 acres; and **Sheep Ridge**, 9,540 acres. These wetlands are difficult to visit because of constant standing water and thick vegetation. However, they can be viewed from forest roads, such as SR 1100, FS 126, and FS 128.

RECREATIONAL OPPORTUNITIES

Hiking and Riding Three major trails, totaling twenty-three miles.

Camping and Picnicking Several areas set aside, on a first-come, first-served basis.

Scenic Drives A number of gravel Forest Service roads skirt the swampy pocosins and explore the Croatan's interior.

Boating and Canoeing Some canoeing and mainly boating on Catfish and Great lakes and on a few other waterways. Brices Creek and White Oak River offer scenic canoeing in upper reaches. Three developed boat ramps provide access to the Neuse and White Oak Rivers and Brices Creek.

Hunting Deer, turkey, quail, and other game. State regulations and licenses apply.

Fishing Freshwater fish include red-breast sunfish, chain pickerel, warmouth, yellow perch, catfish, bluegill, and largemouth bass. Saltwater fishing also popular. Nighttime flounder gigging on the Neuse River. Lake fishing poor because of shallow, acidic water.

Off-Road Vehicles Users should check with Ranger Station for current regulations.

ADMINISTRATIVE OFFICES

Forest Headquarters 100 Otis Street, Box 2750, Asheville, NC 28802 (704) 257-4200

Croatan Ranger District 141 E. Fisher Ave., New Bern, NC 28560 (919) 638-5628

Graceful white azaleas are found in the mountains of South Carolina, home to the Sumter National Forest. Vegetation is starkly different in the coastal Francis Marion National Forest. ADAM JONES

Francis Marion

A N D

Sumter

N A T I O N A L F O R E S T S

*A raging
river and a
swamp fox*

From sea level on the flat Coastal Plain to the southern Appalachian Mountains at nearly 3,300 feet, South Carolina's two national forests encompass the range of the state's topography, vegetation, and wildlife. Recreation possibilities are just as varied. Some of the best white-water boating in the eastern United States can be found in a rocky river tumbling through the Sumter National Forest, while canoeing the mysterious black-water swamps of the Francis Marion National Forest is quieter, but just as engrossing. More than 1.5 million visitors annually pursue these and other activities in the forests, which together cover 607,400 acres, including two sections of the Sumter in the rolling Piedmont hills between the mountains and Atlantic coast.

This patchwork of lands is rich in both history and natural resources, assets considered so vital that people have fought over them since the days of the Indians, through the American Revolution, and into the Civil War. Since 1936, when the two forests were established, the public has owned the bounty of water, wildlife, and trees, and shares their use. In one year, more than sixty million board feet of timber is harvested, with a quarter of the receipts returned to local counties for schools and roads, a practice duplicated throughout the national forest system.

Francis Marion

Hurricane Andrew's rampage across Florida and Louisiana in August of 1992 rekindled painful memories for the people who work in the Francis Marion. Hurricane Hugo turned their world upside down only three years earlier when it struck the coastal forest around midnight on September 21, 1989. Winds up to 135 miles per hour virtually leveled one of the South's most productive pine lands, destroyed its best recreation facilities, and ransacked the rural and town residences where Forest Service employees lived. Personal losses were compounded by the inescapable devastation in the forest. More than 700 million board feet of timber fell in the Francis Marion. Hardest hit were the older, bigger longleaf and loblolly pines, trees crucial to one of the forest's most endangered inhabitants, the red-cockaded woodpecker. Before the hurricane, 2,000

of these birds lived in the Francis Marion, the most concentrated population in the world. Fewer than 600 survived the storm.

As the shock of the disaster subsided, everyone realized that nothing would ever be quite the same again. Trees would be replanted and repairs would be made, but the old Francis Marion was gone. In its place was the challenge to rebuild almost an entire national forest from scratch. Nothing comparable had been done since the 1930s when the Civilian Conservation Corps undertook similar monumental jobs restoring damaged lands into productive forests.

Help came from many other national forests and other sources across the country, from firefighters to smother blazes, to biologists who helped develop and install artificial nesting cavities for the red-cockaded woodpecker. The birds eagerly accepted these alternatives, which are boxes installed in holes cut into surviving pines. In just three years, the woodpecker population climbed to 1,000 and the artificial cavities are being copied elsewhere.

A few forest patches escaped damage, particularly in the northern portion of the Wambaw Ranger District where there is a welcome stretch of unscathed pines. Many old cypress and gums also escaped and still shelter the dark waters of Wambaw Creek Wilderness. Not far away, however, the fishing village of McClellanville and its ranger office were hit hard: shrimp boats were stacked along the shore like toys, and many buildings were damaged. In part to offset revenue loss in timber taxes and jobs, the hurricane's lingering legacies for years to come, a new visitor and environmental education center is planned in McClellanville as a cooperative project between the Forest Service and U.S. Fish and Wildlife Service. Exhibits will explain habitats and wildlife in the Francis Marion National Forest and in nearby Cape Romain

Left: *Trees in the Francis Marion National Forest were snapped at their weakest points by Hurricane Hugo.*
FRED WHITEHEAD
Right: *Alligators silently lurk in the swamps and bayous of the Francis Marion.* WILLIAM J. WEBER

GROWING A FOREST

In a delicate bit of surgery, nursery workers in the Francis Marion Seed Orchard take a cutting from a mature pine that has superior characteristics, such as rapid growth, a straight trunk, or resistance to disease, and graft it onto a year-old seedling. With twice-weekly fertilizing, careful watering, and plenty of sunshine, the result of the operation will be a sturdy specimen to produce superior offspring for the Francis Marion or another southern forest.

The Francis Marion Seed Orchard produces superior trees for the national forests. SHARYN KANE/RICHARD KEETON

Like much of the forest, the orchard was severely damaged by Hurricane Hugo. Over ninety percent of the superior longleaf and loblolly pines were toppled. Replacing them is slow and tedious: cuttings for grafting, for instance, are collected from various national forests from trees about forty-five years old. The replanting of the Francis Marion presents an uncommon opportunity to grow a high percentage of such trees, a bright prospect sparked by a dismal event.

National Wildlife Refuge, where endangered loggerhead sea turtles, shorebirds, and the endangered red wolf live.

Local history will also play a part, including the role of the forest's namesake, Francis Marion, in the American Revolution. Marion and his men harassed British supply lines with surprise attacks, then retreated into the forest's swamps, where dense vegetation and fear of alligators and snakes kept pursuers from following. Dubbed the "Swamp Fox" by his enemies, Marion learned his guerilla tactics by studying Cherokee Indian fighters. Farewell Corner, where the rebels impudently waved goodbye to their foes, can be found on the swamp edge in the forest's Witherbee District.

Long before the Swamp Fox, prehistoric Indians occupied the area and left a large, doughnut-shaped mound of oyster shells as evidence of their gatherings near the salt marsh. This bit of history is part of a new self-guided forest auto tour, along with Battery Warren, an earthen fort built by Confederates to guard the

Santee River during the Civil War. Also new are facilities near the Intracoastal Waterway at Buck Hall Campground, heavily hit by Hugo. Campers and day visitors once again are enjoying boating and casting nets for shrimp close by.

Many species of wildlife find protected habitat in the most recent addition to the forest, South Tibwin Plantation. Few properties left on the coast compare with this 577-acre jewel, consisting of tidal marsh, forests, and ponds. The acquisition is generating great interest as planners envision its potential for habitat, interpretation, and recreation. The future for the plantation, like the rest of the Francis Marion, is full of possibilities.

Sumter

N A T I O N A L   F O R E S T

Life jackets are required for all boaters on the Chattooga River, and helmets are necessary on the more difficult portions. One look at the frothing water crashing over boulders should be enough to convey the wisdom of these precautions. Properly protected, and equipped with either experience or guidance from professional outfitters, floating the Chattooga is an enjoyable challenge for nearly 70,000 people every year. In fact, this wild and scenic river dropping nearly half a mile over its fifty-mile length is the biggest tourist attraction in South Carolina's national forests.

The Chattooga is named for a Cherokee Indian town that existed on its fertile floodplains until the early 1700s (see sidebar story). The river, which today forms the northwestern border of South Carolina with Georgia's Chattahoochee National Forest, begins as a trickle in North Carolina. Steadily gaining size and strength in the Nantahala National Forest, the Chattooga is large enough when it enters South Carolina and Georgia to provide ideal fly fishing opportunities for trout anglers. Boating is prohibited on the upper half of the river (above South Carolina Highway 28) to provide solitude, hiking, and fishing opportunities, with rainbow and brown trout the preferred catch.

The river is fairly calm through the stretch below South Carolina Highway 28, offering recreation for those who want to enjoy the cool water without triggering their adrenaline. This is the second of four delineated river sections and provides moderate challenge (the West Fork of the Chattooga in Georgia is the first section and provides the easiest floating). Even an inner tube can safely navigate the flow that continues at a relaxed pace through most of the second section. From Earl's Ford on, however, where the third section starts, sharp rapids accelerate both the pace of the river and the human response needed to avoid spills. Experienced floaters often pull their rafts ashore, then walk downstream to scout

Rafters find thrills and spills on the Chattooga Wild and Scenic River.
PETE WINKEL/STOCK SOUTH

A Cherokee Indian town of about 100 people bustled on the banks of the Chattooga River until the 1730s. Residents fished in the river, hunted in the surrounding forest, and grew corn and squash in the rich alluvial soils. The villagers governed themselves, holding important meetings and ceremonies in a round, earth-covered building called a townhouse. Here they burned fires for light and heat in a big earthen hearth. The building somehow caught fire and collapsed. Eventually, for unknown reasons, the town ceased to exist.

The history of this town has come to light because of archeological investigations in the Sumter National Forest, where a University of Tennessee professor and students, along with South Carolina public school teachers, have spent four summers peeling back the earth's secrets. Their work on the excavation of the community called Chattooga Old Town is in cooperation with the Forest Service, which seeks to further knowledge about early life on forest lands. Cherokee Indians from North Carolina are among the dedicated workers patiently sifting through soils in search of objects that might reveal more about their ancestors, who once claimed all the eye can see from this abandoned town.

the rapids ahead. Carrying rafts a short distance over land instead of risking a tumble is common, especially in spring, when heavy rains can swell the Chattooga into a thundering torrent. But when conditions are favorable, enthusiasts from many states come to ride one of nature's most exciting roller coasters.

Crews of as many as six share the paddling, with everyone's participation important, because between short spans of relative calm, swift currents bob the raft up and down, spin it around, then push it headlong over steep rock ledges to come crashing down into deep pools. With skill—and luck—riders soon reach a gentler stretch where they invariably erupt into self-congratulating cheers. Conquering the Chattooga seems to stir pride in even the most jaded adventurers.

Hiking and camping attract other visitors to the heavily-wooded corridor on the river's banks. Oaks, hickories, and other hardwoods line the more than fifty miles of nearby trails in the three national forests. In the Andrew Pickens Ranger District of the Sumter, the Foot Hills National Recreation Trail starts at Ocoee State Park and meanders nineteen miles northward through deep coves, past rapids, and along ridges to the North Carolina state line. Burrells Ford Campground, popular with overnight hikers, is near a scenic spur path winding to Kings Creek Falls where water cascades

Great egrets remain nearly motionless while they forage in wetlands. JOE MAC HUDSPETH

65

sixty feet. The trail also passes close to the more developed Cherry Hill Campground farther away from the river. Ellicott Rock Wilderness at the Sumter's northern tip receives the most foot traffic, so those seeking privacy might prefer hiking outside its borders.

Relative seclusion, another sixty-foot waterfall, and an interesting assortment of wildflowers are found on an easy trail through Station Creek Cove Botanical Area, just off State Highway 11. The cove, sheltered by an escarpment, shares features with both the mountains and Piedmont. Spring arrives much sooner to these rich moist soils than to surrounding areas. Spots of color begin poking through the forest floor in March, and sundry blooms continue to appear for months. Among them is the showy orchid, an exquisite white bloom barely an inch big, with a deep purple hood. Trillium, mayapple, wild geranium, and jack-in-the-pulpit are just a few of the other species found.

More of the forest's features can be seen along the Wigginton Scenic Byway (South Carolina State Highway 107), which starts near Oconee State Park and continues northward twelve miles to the North Carolina border. Shortleaf pines, white and red oaks, and hickories grow along the road, while old-growth trees, including South Carolina's largest eastern hemlocks and white pines soaring 160 feet or more, are uncommon features of the Chattooga Picnic Area near Walhalla National Fish Hatchery. The hatchery is open year-round for free tours.

The Sumter's two Piedmont divisions are widely separated but similar, with pines dominating the gentle slopes. Gaping scars, however, still mar some areas, reminders of when cotton was king. Before the national forests were established, cotton exhausted soils and farmers lost or abandoned the land, which sometimes eroded into deep gullies. For years, forest managers have been restoring the damage. In some cases, sawtooth oaks are planted and protected in tubular plastic "tree shelters" until they are strongly rooted. Eventually the oaks will bear acorns, another wildlife food staple. The trees grow rapidly, adding several feet per year, and before long a former gully begins to resemble a natural forest. ♣

Francis Marion
NATIONAL FOREST DIRECTORY

POINTS OF INTEREST

Red-Cockaded Woodpecker Look for trees with two white paint bands to identify cavity nesting sites for the endangered birds. Early morning and sunset are best observation times.

Wildflowers More than forty orchid species thrive in the forest. Carnivorous pitcher plants and sundews are found here, as well as many other species.

McClellanville Picturesque fishing village with shrimp boats, art galleries, old churches, and quaint restaurants welcomes visitors. Wambaw District Ranger Station in town has guidebooks and other forest information.

Hampton Plantation State park with historical 1750s home. Off Highway 857-S.

WILDERNESS AREAS

Hell Hole Bay 2,125 acres, mostly wet, is traversed by an interesting trail, used for canoeing during high water and hiking during droughts. No recovery work will be done in this or other wildernesses hit by the hurricane, so foot travel, always difficult, is even more challenging.

Wambaw Creek 1,825 acres. Canoeing makes this the most accessible of forest's wilderness areas. A corridor about eleven miles long protects the fascinating black waters of Wambaw Creek, influenced by ocean tides. Barred owls, alligators, and many other species may be seen.

Wambaw Swamp 4,815 acres. No trails. Compass strongly advised.

Little Wambaw Swamp 5,047 acres of bottomland hardwoods and sloughs. Wading often required.

RECREATIONAL OPPORTUNITIES

Hiking and Riding Swamp Fox National Recreation Trail is an easy twenty-mile hiking and bicycling path connecting the two ranger districts. Jericho Trail, nineteen miles, open to horses, mountain bikes and hikers, crosses several scenic bridges. Wambaw Motorcycle Trail is a popular forty-mile figure-eight loop that is also open to mountain bikes.

Camping Buck Hall Recreation Area on the Intracoastal Waterway is most developed for picnicking, boating, and camping. Also four primitive camping areas.

Hunting White-tailed deer, turkey, and other game. Licenses issued by South Carolina Wildlife and Marine Resources Department.

Fishing Saltwater fishing popular near Buck Hall Recreation Area, and in Santee River and Awendaw Creek. Ponds across the forest are stocked with bass, bluegill, and shellcrackers. Licenses issued by South Carolina Wildlife and Marine Resources Department.

Rifle Ranges Twin Ponds and Boggy Head are free ranges open daily.

Boating Six launching ramps across the forest.

Swimming Forest's only swimming area is at Canal Picnic Area, located on the forest's western edge on Highway 52.

Off-Road Vehicles Allowed, with restrictions. Get map from ranger office.

ADMINISTRATIVE OFFICES

Forest Headquarters 1835 Assembly St., Room 333, Strom Thurmond Building, Columbia, SC 29201 (803)765-5222

Witherbee Ranger Station HC 69, Box 1532, Moncks Corner, SC 29461 (803) 336-3248

Wambaw Ranger Station P. O. Box 788, McClellanville, SC 29458 (803)887-3257

Sumter
NATIONAL FOREST DIRECTORY

POINTS OF INTEREST

Chattooga River Information Site Outdoor exhibit near Highway 76 Bridge. Short walk to the river and good observation point for watching rafters.

Chauga River Scenic Area Less-known, smaller, but equally rugged river flows through a gorge in a 3,275 scenic area south of Highway 193.

Station Cove Botanical Area Wildflowers bloom early in a protected cove near a waterfall off State Highway 11.

WILDERNESS AREAS

Ellicott Rock 9,012 acres spread over South Carolina, Georgia, and North Carolina. Chattooga River's scenic east fork flows through the 2,809 acres in South Carolina.

RECREATIONAL OPPORTUNITIES

Hiking and Riding Heaviest use occurs on fifty-seven miles of mountain trails, many of which pass near scenic waters and over rugged terrain. Equestrians can ride the twelve miles of loop trails on the Rocky Gap Trail in South Carolina, and can ford Chattooga River to extend their ride on the seventeen-mile-long Wilson Knob Trail in Georgia. Hikers, equestrians and bicyclists share two piedmont district trails, Buncombe and Long Cane, both over twenty miles. Easy to difficult off-road vehicle trails found throughout the Sumter. Parson's Mountain and Cedar Springs Motorcycle Trails span twenty-two miles near Greenwood in Long Cane Ranger District. The newly completed Enofer O.R.V. Trail provides miles of riding opportunity near Whitmire.

Camping Four major campgrounds (Cherry Hill, Parson Mountain, Lick Fork and Woods Ferry) provide 100 sites. Also twenty-nine primitive sites used primarily by hunters. Toilet and trash facilities provided at all campsites; drinking water available at most.

McClellanville harbors many shrimp boats.
SHARYN KANE/RICHARD KEETON

Scenic Drives South Carolina State 107 starts near Oconee State Park and continues northward to the North Carolina border for twelve miles as the Wigginton Scenic Byway.

Rafting, Kayaking, and Canoeing Twenty-eight miles of the Wild and Scenic Chattooga River rated easy to extremely difficult. Outfitters provide training and equipment. Piedmont canoeing poplar on Tyger and Enoree Rivers, Stevens and Long Cane Creek.

Hunting White-tailed deer, turkey, squirrels, and other game. Licenses issued by South Carolina Wildlife and Marine Resources Department.

Fishing Excellent river, stream, and pond fishing throughout the forest. Trout, bass, and catfish popular sport fish. Licenses issued by South Carolina Wildlife and Marine Resources Department.

Rifle Ranges Seven free ranges generally open daily across the forest for pistol and rifle practice.

Off-Road Vehicles Allowed on ORV trails, with restrictions. Obtain map from ranger offices.

ADMINISTRATIVE OFFICES

Forest Headquarters Strom Thurmond Federal Building, 1835 Assembly St., Room 333, Columbia, SC 29201 (803) 765-5222

Andrew Pickens Ranger Station 112 Andrew Pickens Circle, Mountain Rest, SC 29664 (803) 638-9568

Edgefield Ranger Station 321 Bacon St., Box 30, Edgefield, SC 29824 (803) 637-5396

Enoree Ranger Station Route 1, Box 179, Whitmire, SC 29178 (803) 276-4810

Long Cane Ranger Station Room 201, Federal Building, Box 3168, Greenwood, SC 29646, (803) 229-2406

Tyger Ranger Station Drawer 10, Union, SC 29379 (803) 427-9858

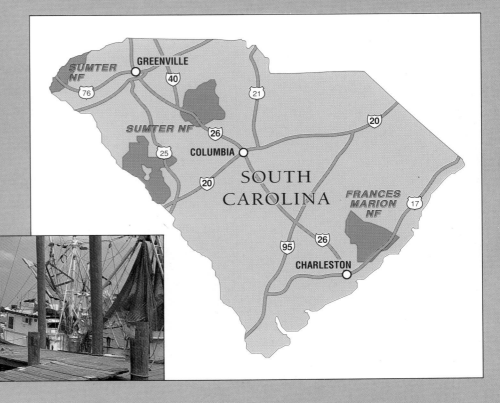

Years have passed since panthers were sighted in north Georgia, but Panther Creek continues to flow through the Chattahoochee National Forest. The Chattahoochee spreads across the breadth of the state. Waterfalls are among the forest's best-known attractions, along with miles of hiking trails and ten wilderness areas. CRAIG M. TANNER

Chattahoochee
AND
Oconee

N A T I O N A L   F O R E S T S

Hiking haven

A painter captivated by the play of light across a landscape might never want to leave the DeSoto Falls Recreation Area in the Chattahoochee National Forest. Dappled sunlight catches and magnifies the rich greens and browns of the lush hardwood forest in summer, and illuminates the white rhododendron blossoms as big as snowballs. When the sun reaches a stream rippling beside a trail, the water sparkles like liquid jewels.

The visual banquet continues as the trail climbs steadily higher, and one of three large waterfalls comes into view. Two lovers, their arms around each other's waists, stand on a platform built out over the rocks and stare for a long moment at the rushing cascade.

Perhaps, as legend contends, Spanish conquistador Hernando de Soto stopped here to drink the cool waters in his futile search for gold. Then again, maybe he didn't. His route is the subject of great scholarly debate. Historians are certain that DeSoto never found any of the rich gold deposits in the Georgia mountains that centuries later stirred frenzied mining around the town of Dahlonega. Panning for nuggets in the many streams continues today, and every fall, Dahlonega citizens commemorate their town's gilded past with a gold rush days festival.

DeSoto Falls Recreation Area is located off U.S. 19

and 129, a snaking, two-lane road typical of the highways in the Georgia portions of the Appalachian Mountains. Frequent sharp curves demand alert drivers, while passengers are free to enjoy spectacular vistas that seem to be around every bend in the Chattahoochee National Forest, which extends across the region for 750,000 acres.

Continuing north, the road reaches Walasi-Yi Interpretive Center, a wood and stone building erected by the Civilian Conservation Corps. The center, owned by the state of Georgia, has the distinction of being the only place where the Appalachian Trail passes through a building. Hikers walk through a stone breezeway next to the center store where mountain crafts and other items are sold.

The famous 2,135-mile trail begins in the Chattahoochee to the southwest at Springer Mountain, beyond Blood Mountain, at 4,458 feet the highest peak

the path reaches in Georgia. The new Ed Jenkins National Recreation Area on Springer Mountain will likely increase the already significant numbers of visitors drawn to the crest.

To the east of Walasi-Yi Center, the trail enters Raven Cliff Wilderness, one of five Chattahoochee wilderness areas along its seventy-nine miles in Georgia. These are some of the most challenging miles on the entire Appalachian Trail, and for more than a few hikers who set out to walk all the way to Maine, the Georgia stretch proves to be far enough after all.

As the Chattahoochee sprawls westward across almost the entire width of north Georgia, it is in-

Above: *The stealthy bobcat, his fur blending with his surroundings, usually foils attempts to spot him.*
BILL LEA
Right: *Besides oaks, poplars, and hickories, evergreens are also found in the Chattahoochee, including hemlocks and pines. Hardscrabble farms dot the valleys between the wooded mountain peaks.* DAVID MOLCHOS

terrupted by a broad gap of private land and towns called the Great Valley. Past this low ground, the forest resumes on the other side of Interstate 75 in a stretch of mountains different from those to the east. In this western sector, peaks are lower and shaped in long, narrow ridges, separated by valleys. The valleys create a natural entrance into Georgia and have been used for centuries as human and animal passageways. Great armies clashed here during the Civil War as Union General William Tecumseh Sherman led his troops towards the fateful battle of Atlanta, which sealed the Confederacy's doom.

Part of the extended Ridge and Valley Province of the great Appalachians, the high ground in the western sector of the Chattahoochee is called the Armuchee Ridges. "Armuchee" is a Cherokee Indian word meaning "land of flowers," still an accurate description for parts of the forest. Dainty Queen Anne's lace is common, as well as other wildflowers.

Although not nearly as heavily traveled as the eastern reaches of the forest, this part of the Chattahoochee just south of Chattanooga, Tennessee, has its share of attractions. Rock hounds hunt for fossils in the predominately sedimentary rocks laid down by ancient seas.

The Ridge and Valley Scenic Byway tours the region in a forty-seven mile loop. A highlight is the John's Mountain Overlook where the view reaches into Alabama and Tennessee. A nature trail from the overlook connects with another trail leading to Keown Falls Scenic Area where twin waterfalls can be enjoyed from an observation platform. Common farther east, waterfalls are unusual in northwestern Georgia, and even Keown Falls sometimes disappears in extended dry spells. Similarly, nearby Hidden Creek flows on some days and vanishes on others.

Heading back east from the Armuchee Ridges across the Great Valley, the ground rises sharply in the Blue Ridge Mountains. Here, soon after the forest begins again, lies Lake Conasauga, the state's highest lake at more than 3,000 feet. The water is surrounded by white pines, easily identified by limbs that grow in orderly wagon-wheel rows. Eastern hemlocks are mixed among the pines, and for both species, Georgia marks the farthest point south where they appear.

The lake is often quiet and uncrowded and a good spot for catching bass and other fish. The swimming beach is popular among summer visitors from nearby towns and the adjacent Forest Service campground. Travel to the lake is over a dirt and gravel road that shrinks to little more than a single lane in places.

The Conasauga Songbird Management Area is close by and is fast becoming a magnet for birdwatchers. The Forest Service has set aside 120 acres around beaver ponds and a stream to create inviting habitat for migrating songbirds along the Appalachian flyway. Small stands of trees were cut to encourage growth of edible plants favored by various birds. So far, a total of 138 bird species have been counted here. A trail circles the area, and, depending on the season, a hiker may sight rose-breasted grosbeaks, pine siskins, scarlet tanagers,

and some of the many vireos that rest and feed in this special retreat. All told, the Chattahoochee, combined with the Oconee National Forest in central Georgia, provides significant habitat for over 500 wildlife and fish species.

Lake Conasauga Recreation Area borders the Cohutta Wilderness, the largest wilderness in the Southeast at more than 37,000 acres (part of this wilderness extends into Tennessee's Cherokee National Forest). Sixteen trails offer more than ninety miles of hiking through the Cohutta. Some paths are fairly easy and several are suitable for horseback riding. Others, however, are decidedly difficult. Tearbritches Trail, for example, lives up to its name, and Jack's River and Conasauga River Trails meander repeatedly across streams. Knowing hikers expect to get their feet wet

and carry extra shoes.

East of the Cohutta across another valley, Big Bald Mountain soars to 4,000 feet in the Rich Mountain Wilderness. This wilderness is less known than the Cohutta, but equally engaging, with opportunities to see many plants normally found only much farther north.

Lake Blue Ridge nearby is the only place in Georgia where anglers can catch muskellunge, or muskie. The 3,290-acre lake is bordered by two Forest Service

Left: Now commonly found growing wild, oxeye daisies were introduced from Europe. These flowers favor bright sun and often grow along roadsides. BILL LEA

Above right: The blue-winged warbler's melodious song is usually heard near forest edges and clearings. F.D. ATWOOD

Below: Birdwatchers find much to see in the Chattahoochee at the Lake Conasauga Songbird Management Area. SHARYN KANE/ RICHARD KEETON

campgrounds, privately-owned lodging, and a marina that rents boats. Nottely Lake, Lake Chatuge, Lake Burton, and Lake Rabun also touch the Chattahoochee, and provide similar opportunities for boating, swimming, and fishing. There are also over 1,000 miles of trout streams in the forest.

Canoeists favor Toccoa River, which, unlike most Georgia rivers, flows north instead of south. The Toccoa, considered by many to be the state's loveliest river, empties into Lake Blue Ridge, then flows on into Tennessee and becomes the Ocoee River.

Old-growth trees are the inducements to visit Cooper Creek Scenic Area, southeast of Lake Blue Ridge.

This special enclave shelters enormous white and Northern red oaks, black birches, and tulip poplars. In a section called the Valley of the Giants, poplars are especially large, with diameters spanning six feet.

Cooper Creek has long been preferred by anglers. Lake Winfield Scott, the source of Cooper Creek, is noted for rainbow trout, with camping and hiking popular along the shores. Near the lake, Sosebee Cove Scenic Area is dedicated to Arthur Woody, an early forest ranger. Established in 1936, the Chattahoochee National Forest was heavily logged and over-hunted like most other woodlands in the South before the Forest Service became the stewards. Woody spent his own money to reintroduce white-tailed deer into the Chattahoochee after hunters nearly eliminated them in the late 1800s. The rare yellowwood tree with its fragrant white blossoms is one of the many tree species found here. Coosa Bald National Scenic Area northwest of the cove climbs 4,271 feet and is part of Duncan Ridge, which is crossed by several challenging hiking trails.

Driving through the

Chattahoochee to see the fall leaves is an annual ritual for thousands, and few routes are as colorful as the Russell-Brasstown Scenic Byway. One starting point for the thirty-eight-mile loop is near Helen, a small tourist town with Bavarian building facades. From Helen, the byway follows State Highway 348, also called the Russell-Brasstown Scenic Byway along this stretch. Dukes Creek Falls is one of many possible stops along the way. A steep walkway leads for almost a mile to the bottom of a gorge, where the air is moist and cool from the spray of the falls. Hikers often reward themselves with a swim in the cold water that tumbles for 250 feet over rocks and forms several pools. Visitors are cautioned that the walkway is the safest path for enjoying the falls. Many injuries and some fatalities have occurred when visitors have ventured off the path into the very slippery areas at the top and along the sides of the falls.

Farther along the drive reaches a trailhead for Raven Cliffs Falls Trail. The path twists for two-and-a-half miles around several waterfalls in Raven Cliffs Wilderness, including one of the most unusual falls in the forest where water pours out of a crevice in a massive cliff some ninety feet tall.

Another interesting stop is Brasstown Bald, Georgia's highest peak at 4,784 feet. Shuttle vans carry most visitors from a parking lot to the top, but there are also fair numbers of hikers following a path to the crest. Winds are ever present on the lofty summit, which on clear days offers a breathtaking panorama of mountains and valleys. A Forest Service visitor center features multimedia exhibits about the Chattahoochee, with books, gifts, and refreshments for sale.

Several trails suitable for day hikes travel across Brasstown Bald, including the Arkaquah Trail, which descends for 5.5 miles through Brasstown Bald Wilderness to Track Rock Gap Archeological Area. Here, prehistoric Indians carved rock petroglyphs of circles, footprints, and other shapes. The seven-mile Wagon

Train Trail shows off Brasstown Bald's boulder fields and cliffs. Huge yellow birch trees draped in old-man's beard lichen grow along the way, and small violets and trilliums poke their colorful heads up through the ground leaf cover.

Another visitor center and gift shop is located just off the byway near one of the most frequently visited sites in the forest, Anna Ruby Falls. A short paved trail leads to an observation platform at the base of the twin falls.

Fewer people find their way to the northern edge of the Chattahoochee where another scenic drive travels through the Upper Tallulah Basin, a place of stark beauty. Forest Road 70 skirts the Tallulah River that carved a deep chasm through the rock. Near Tate Branch Campground, look for a cluster of rare mountain camellia trees. In summer, the trees open white blossoms similar to a magnolia's. Also along the road, there is access to a mile-long trail to Coleman River Scenic Area, where there are waterfalls and more mountain camellia trees.

The designated Wild and Scenic Chattooga River forms the forest's eastern border, and can be more exciting than an amusement park when rafters challenge the rapids during high water. Outfitters offer equipment and guides. Several long hiking trails are also nearby, including the Bartram and Chattooga Trails. These, however, are just a few of the dozens of extended footpaths that make the Chattahoochee a hiker's mecca.

If a wealth of trails is the hallmark of the Chattahoochee, bountiful game is the signature of the Oconee, where there are fifty hunt camps in a forest of only about 100,000 acres. Deer and turkey are the principal game, but there are also good squirrel and quail populations. Fishing is also excellent, particularly in the Ocmulgee River where spring catches of red-breast sunfish are considered exceptional.

The Oconee is separated into two principal sections by Interstate 20 and is a relatively young national forest, established in 1959. Unlike the tall peaks of the Chattahoochee, the Oconee terrain is mostly flat with small hills here and there. Once mostly eroded farmland, soils are healthy again and nourish strong stands of pines, including the loblolly, preferred nesting habitat for the endangered red-cockaded woodpecker. Pro-

Above Left: A visitor center sits atop Brasstown Bald. BILL CLARK/STOCK SOUTH
Left: Mountain ash trees with red fruit are visible from Brasstown Bald, Georgia's highest peak. DAVID MOLCHOS
Right: A hungry whitetail buck browses tulip poplar leaves. BILL LEA

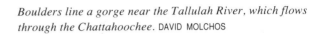
Boulders line a gorge near the Tallulah River, which flows through the Chattahoochee. DAVID MOLCHOS

ductive timberland, the Oconee contributes its fair share of the sixty million board feet harvested annually in the two forests.

Water is an important feature in the two principal recreation areas. Lake Sinclair, 15,300 acres, is popular for swimming, fishing, and boating, and has a lakeshore campground and hiking trail. The Oconee River Campground is a favorite launching point for canoeing on the river, which leads to Lake Oconee, known for its crappie and other fish. There is also an easy one-mile trail starting at the campground to one of Georgia's ghost towns, Scull Shoals. Crumbling walls and other ruins stand as reminders of the people who once worked in the state's first cotton gin and paper mill. Another short trail nearby leads to two ceremonial mounds built by prehistoric Indians. ♠

Chattahoochee
NATIONAL FOREST DIRECTORY

POINTS OF INTEREST

Coleman River Scenic Area Large hemlock trees and rare mountain camellias. Located along a scenic drive through the upper Tallulah Basin, the area can be reached by driving west from Clayton on U. S. Hwy. 76 for about eight miles. Turn right on an unnumbered paved county road and drive four miles. Turn left onto Forest Road 70 and go a little over a mile to the Coleman River Bridge and the trailhead.

Brasstown Bald Georgia's highest peak at 4,784 feet. A recently updated Visitor Center offers multi-media exhibits. Books, Appalachian pottery, and refreshments are available at the log cabin gift shop. Several trails from near the summit cross the Brasstown Wilderness. Take State Hwy. 75/17 north from Helen. Turn left on State Hwy.180 and go about six miles. Turn right on State Hwy. 180 spur that climbs the mountain. A hiking trail also leads from the beginning of this spur road up the mountain.

Lake Conasauga Songbird Management Area A high-altitude site visited by more than 100 bird species. From Ellijay, take State Hwy. 52 west for seven miles to Forest Road 18. Follow this paved road and keep going when the pavement ends. Turn right on Forest Road 68 and drive for about ten miles.

Lake Russell Recreation Area Uncrowded campground in the rolling hill country just south of the mountains. Located on a 100-acre lake, the campground also is near several trails, including the six-mile Ladyslipper Trail for hikers and horseback riders. From Cornelia, take U.S. Hwy. 123

north and east about one-and-a-half miles. At Mount Airy, turn right on Forest Road 59, then go two miles.

WILDERNESS AREAS

Blood Mountain 7,800 acres.

Mark Trail 16,400 acres.

Brasstown Bald 12,565 acres.

Cohutta 35,247 acres in Georgia.

Ellicott Rock 2,181 acres in Georgia.

Southern Nantahala 11,770 acres in Georgia.

Raven Cliffs 8,562 acres.

Tray Mountain 9,702 acres.

Rich Mountain 9,649 acres.

Big Frog Eighty-three acres in Georgia.

RECREATIONAL OPPORTUNITIES

Hiking and Riding Hundreds of miles of hiking trails, including the Appalachian, Benton MacKaye, Bartram, and Duncan Ridge long-distance trails. Various trails also accommodate horseback riding.

Camping Developed campgrounds are located throughout the forest. Dispersed camping is also allowed in most areas.

Scenic Drives Many roads have outstanding views, including the Ridge and Valley Scenic Byway and the Russell-Brasstown Scenic Byway.

Rafting, Kayaking, and Canoeing The Chattooga Wild and Scenic River is the most popular for whitewater trips. A number of other streams, including the Chattahoochee and Toccoa Rivers, are also floated.

Rock Climbing One of the most popular spots is Yonah Mountain near Cleveland.

Hunting Deer, turkey, squirrel, ruffed grouse, and other game. State licenses required. There are thirteen wildlife management areas where hunting seasons may vary from state seasons.

Fishing Over 1,367 miles of primary trout streams and 112 miles of secondary trout streams. Also good fishing for muskie, walleye, bluegill, bass, and others. State licenses and regulations apply.

Off-Road Vehicles Just about every section of the forest has areas or trails set aside. Check with ranger stations for maps and regulations.

ADMINISTRATIVE OFFICES

Forest Headquarters 508 Oak Street, Gainesville, GA 30501 (404) 536-0541

Armuchee Ranger District 806 East Villanow, P. O. Box 465, LaFayette, GA 30728 (706) 638-1085

Brasstown Ranger District Hwy. 19 and 129 South, P. O. Box 9, Blairsville, GA 30512 (706) 745-6928

Chattooga Ranger District Hwy. 197, Burton Road, P. O. Box 196, Clarkesville, GA 30523 (706) 754-6221

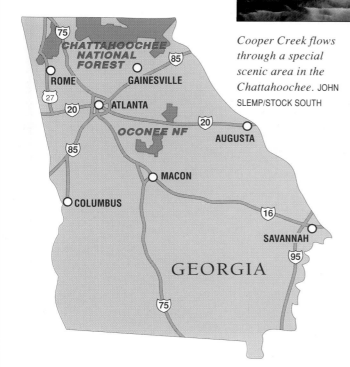

Cooper Creek flows through a special scenic area in the Chattahoochee. JOHN SLEMP/STOCK SOUTH

Chestatee Ranger District 1015 Tipton Drive, Dahlonega, GA 30533 (706) 864-6173

Cohutta Ranger District 401 Old Ellijay Road, Chatsworth, GA 30705 (706) 695-6736

Tallulah Ranger District P. O. Box 438, Clayton, GA 30525 (706) 782-3320

Toccoa Ranger District Suite 5, Owenby Building, East Main Street, Blue Ridge, GA 30513 (706) 632-3031

Oconee
NATIONAL FOREST DIRECTORY

POINTS OF INTEREST

Lake Sinclair Recreation Area Popular campground on the shores of a 15,330-acre lake. Take U.S. Hwy. 129 from Eatonton south for about ten miles. Turn left on State Hwy. 212 for one mile, then left on Forest Road 1062.

Oconee River Recreation Area Campground with a hiking trail leading to Scull Shoals, one of Georgia's ghost towns. From Greensboro, just north of Interstate 20, take State Hwy. 15 northwest for about twelve miles.

RECREATIONAL OPPORTUNITIES

Hiking and Riding There are hiking trails near major recreation areas. Three trails are suitable for horseback riding near the Ocmulgee River. Horseback riding is also permitted on the one-mile Burgess Mountain Trail near Eatonton, which reaches the highest point on the forest at 645 feet.

Camping Dispersed camping is allowed in much of the forest. Fifty hunt camps scattered throughout the forest are useful during hunting and fishing seasons.

Canoeing Float trips are possible in several areas.

Hunting Deer, turkey, squirrel, quail, and other game. State licenses required. There are two wildlife management areas and the Hitchiti Experimental Forest where hunting seasons may differ from state seasons.

Fishing Red-breast sunfish, crappie, and other fish. State regulations and license apply.

Off-Road Vehicle The Town Creek Trail north of Greensboro is fifteen miles long and designated primarily for motorbikes. All-terrain vehicles, however, also use the trail.

ADMINISTRATIVE OFFICES

Forest Headquarters 508 Oak Street, Gainesville, GA 30501 (404) 536-0541

Oconee Ranger District 349 Forsyth Street, Monticello, GA 31064 (706) 468-2244

The Timucuan Nature Trail in the Ocala National Forest is named for Native Americans who once occupied the land. Illustrated trail markers provide details about how these early people used the plants and trees in their daily lives. Located near Alexander Springs, the path crosses through several distinct ecosystems. FRED WHITEHEAD

Florida

Ocala · Osceola · Apalachicola

N A T I O N A L   F O R E S T S

Crystalline waters and deep woods

Warm weather, scenic beaches, and exotic subtropical plants and wildlife have long made Florida one of the nation's most popular vacation destinations. But as traditional tourist spots become more crowded and exploding development consumes dwindling green space, visitors and Florida residents alike are increasingly turning to the national forests. About three million people annually visit the Apalachicola, Osceola, and Ocala, enjoying activities uncommon in national forests, from scuba diving in pristine springs to hiking through alligator territory. The forests cover more than 1,135,306 acres, and over 400,000 of those are wetlands, which produce about 600 billion gallons of water each year. Not surprisingly, water sports are especially popular with 36,000 acres of lakes and ponds, countless creeks and streams, and many rivers, including the Sopchoppy and Ochlockonee, both under review for wild and scenic designation.

The forests' appeal also extends to hikers on 362 miles of hiking and riding trails, some passing through remnants of the dwindling subtropical wilderness along the Florida National Scenic Trail. The trail, cut through sections of stunning visual and biological diversity on the forests, will eventually span the entire length and breadth of the state. Volunteers help maintain this and other forest trails, one of many ways that mounting public interest in enhancing recreation is helping meet growing demands on the forests' resources.

While recreation draws most visitors, all three forests are working forests, each with a history of providing resources and jobs for nearly a century. Permits are issued for beekeepers to maintain hives on all the forests, while farmers graze cattle on the Apalachicola and Osceola. Less familiar, perhaps, is the work of worm grunting. A grunter pushes a stick into the ground, then creates vibrations by rubbing it with a metal rod; worms forced to the surface by the disturbance are then collected and sold.

But harvesting timber is by far the dominant commercial venture. Twenty-five percent of the gross receipts from the national forests is returned annually to local counties for schools and roads. A total of sixty-three animals and fifty plants listed as endangered, threatened, or sensitive species live within Florida's national forests, from the well-known manatee to the more obscure Florida bonamia wildflower. Balancing the needs of wildlife against those of visitors seeking fun and relaxation and others seeking a livelihood is the escalating challenge.

Ocala

N A T I O N A L F O R E S T

Hundreds of millions of gallons of water bubbles daily from artesian springs spread across the Ocala in central Florida, providing a constant flow of clear refreshment beneath an often searing subtropical sun. While scuba divers explore underwater, children play on the beach beside Alexander Springs near an ancient

mound of freshwater shells left by prehistoric Indians. Not far away, at Silver Glen Springs, another prehistoric shell heap is found. The famous early naturalist, William Bartram, wrote about this shell mound in the late 1700s. Bartram also described the unusual plant life and abundant birds and animals he observed, a

pleasure that can still be enjoyed. Silver Glen Springs teems with fish, attracting many birds, including the stately great blue heron.

Rising from limestone caverns, the springs understandably are the best-known sights of the Ocala. Established in 1908, this is one of the oldest national forests east of the Mississippi River. Within a few hours drive of Disney World and other tourist spots, the Ocala draws millions of visitors annually to its 383,000 acres, which contain central highlands, coastal lowlands, swamps, and hundreds of lakes and ponds. Another river, the black-water Ocklawaha, forms the forest's western border and is a favorite of canoers who can float with little obstruction for more than twenty miles.

Deep porous sand ridges, deposited by seas during the Pleistocene era, support the world's largest sand pine-scrub oak ecosystem, sheltering such species as the gopher tortoise and threatened scrub jay. The Ocala's sand pines—tall, spindly trees that noticeably bend and often topple from their own weight—are harvested primarily for pulpwood and are one of the few trees that grow to merchantable size in the arid sand. The climate makes the Ocala especially popular in winter, particularly among retired northern visitors, locally called "snowbirds." But full-time Floridians also flock to the Ocala, much of which is easily accessible because of State Highway 40, which cuts through the middle of the forest and divides the two ranger districts, the Lake George and the Seminole. Contemporary visitors travel in the footsteps of Indians of 10,000 years ago, who were followed by the Spanish in the 1500s, and ultimately by American settlers after President

Andrew Jackson bought the Florida Territory in 1821. The Ocala historically has been used for hunting and fishing, as well as logging and turpentining.

The range of activities available is as diverse as the environment, from canoeing in slow, clear waters, to exploring four wilderness areas. Fishing is excellent, particularly for bass, while hunting white-tailed deer is also popular. Camping is permitted year-round at both developed sites that can accommodate large recre-

Left: The Ocala's pristine Silver Glen Springs is ideal for underwater exploring. FRED WHITEHEAD
Above right: The common moorhen or gallinule feeds on the edges of springs and lakes. JOHN SHAW
Right: Juniper Springs is a popular swimming spot with perpetual fresh water flowing from the earth.
FRED WHITEHEAD

ational vehicles, as well as more primitive areas suitable only for tents. Dispersed camping is allowed in many parts of the forest, except during hunting season, and is common along the sixty-six miles of the Florida National Scenic Trail, which travels the length of the Ocala. The trail twists through many of the forest's most visually dramatic sections, passing over boardwalks through swamps, skirting close to several springs, and cutting through the middle of the Juniper Prairie Wilderness. The prairies here are reminiscent of Midwestern tallgrass prairies, forming first as water spots, then gradually filling with sediments and vegetation. Various pines and oaks rim the prairies, often with an understory of dense palmetto. A place of both historical and literary interest, Pat's Island, is within the Juniper Prairie Wilderness. Pat's Island is not a landmass surrounded by water, but an oasis of longleaf pine and oak scrub fringed by a sea of dry sand pine scrub. It was named for farmer Patrick Smith, whom Marjorie Kinnan Rawlings visited. She used this isolated spot as the setting for "The Yearling," her Pulitzer Prize-winning novel of 1939. A trail passes through the former homestead.

Another spot of historical interest is Juniper Springs, where the Civilian Conservation Corps built a picturesque waterwheel in the mid-1930s to generate electricity. Although no longer used for power, the waterwheel still turns. In a building adjoining the wheel, visitors can review the history of the springs, which had degenerated into a mudhole before restoration. The site is heavily used and swimming is especially popular in the springs, which have been shared for years with an eel. There is also an interpretive trail.

Less frequented but equally appealing are recreation sites on the western side of the forest at Fore Lake and Lake Eaton. There are observation platforms on the water at Lake Eaton along a trail that passes through sand pine scrub and oak hammocks. "Hammock" is thought to be derived from an Indian word meaning "shady place," an apt description for the lush greenery of live oaks, magnolias, hickories, dogwoods, sabal palms, and loblolly pines found in the base of the Lake Eaton Sinkhole, on another trail nearby. Unlike many deep sinks, this one has not filled with water despite its depth of eighty feet. Stairs to the bottom provide a close look into an ecosystem rare in the midst of a sand pine forest.

The Timucuan Nature Trail presents more information about the Ocala's diverse vegetation—and its many human uses. Named for Indians who once occupied the area, the short trail with interpretive signs is an easy hike beside Alexander Springs. Look for the startling resurrection fern. Brown and withered during droughts, the fern springs to vivid life after a rain, a fitting metaphor for the Ocala, a place both intensely hot and dry, and refreshingly cool and wet.

The Civilian Conservation Corps built this waterwheel to generate electricity. The wheel still turns at Juniper Springs, located in the Ocala National Forest.
GLENN VAN NIMWEGEN

Osceola

Before the Osceola was established in 1931, much of its pine woods and cypress swamps west of Jacksonville were scarred from timber cutting, then abandoned—but systematic replanting by the Forest Service with careful harvesting have caused a resurgence. Considered a "flatwoods" because of little elevation variation on its 181,000 acres, the Osceola's significance is only partly shaped by longleaf and slash pines. Almost one-half of the forest is vital wetlands, including Pinhook Swamp, an extension of the legendary Okefenokee Swamp in Georgia. Pinhook Swamp helps form headwaters of the Suwannee and St. Mary's Rivers, and provides important habitat for wildlife, from sandhill cranes to black bear.

While hundreds of motorists on Interstate 10 drive through the Osceola daily, most pass unaware of the recreational opportunities and historical significance surrounding them. Nearby residents, however, take frequent advantage of the Osceola's main developed site, Ocean Pond, a 1,760-acre natural lake. Graceful pond cypress trees trailing gray wisps of Spanish moss dot the circular shoreline of Ocean Pond, named not for any marine connection, but for occasional churning waves. Like Osceola's swamps, Ocean Pond is the hue of strong tea because of tannic acid leaching from vegetation. The acid is harmless and has no effect on fishing, swimming, or on water skiing in the lake. There are two main boat ramps, one at Ocean Pond campground and another at Olustee Beach,

the day-use area. A less developed boat ramp is also available at Hog Pen Landing.

Civil War buffs may recognize the name Olustee as the site of a bloody clash between Union and Confederate soldiers, a battle reenacted by uniformed enthusiasts every February close to the date it occurred (see sidebar story). The battlefield, now within the Osceola's boundaries, is commemorated by a monument and museum within a few yards of the eastern start of the forest's twenty-one-mile stretch of the Florida National Scenic Trail.

Hikers experience a view strikingly different than the docile environment around Ocean Pond. The Seminole Indian Warrior for whom the forest is named would not feel out of place on the trail, wandering

Pines, palmettos, and wetlands blanket the landscape of the Osceola National Forest.
MARK J. BARRETT/STOCK SOUTH

AT OLUSTEE BATTLEFIELD

A bloody Civil War battle is commemorated with a museum and monuments.
SHARYN KANE/RICHARD KEETON

"It was a fair, square, stand-up fight in pine woods...." So began the diary entry of Colonel Joseph Hawley, as he recounted the awful fight involving more than 10,000 men at Olustee between his Union soldiers and the Confederates. Yankee forces, attempting to secure important supply links, were stopped at Olustee by the Rebels, who chose the pine forest for the battle stage. Fighting raged throughout the day of February 20, 1864, until, with the coming of darkness, the defeated Union soldiers retreated. Nearly 3,000 were killed, and oral tradition says that surviving comrades buried many of the dead beneath the pines, carving the soldiers' names into the trees as their tombstones.

The Olustee Battlefield State Historic Site is open year-round, Thursday through Monday, free of charge, and offers both pictorial and written histories of Florida's biggest and most famous Civil War battle. Uniforms and equipment typical of the period are shown, and there is also a trail marking the battlefield. Since 1970, enthusiasts from across the country have played out the struggle on the site every year. For more information, contact Olustee Battlefield State Historic Site, P. O. Box 40, Olustee, FL 32702 (904) 752-3866.

where wild turkeys roost and white-tailed deer browse among huckleberry bushes. Despite its seemingly undisturbed state, segments are blazed on old railroad beds, used around the turn of the century. Rail beds remain as visible ridges in spots, along with a few ties.

Signs of another early industry also exist. Until the late 1940s, tapping pine trees—or turpentining—was common. Tapping involved slashing through bark to bleed natural resins into cups attached to the trees. Both the practice and trees were known as naval stores because predominant customers were operators of sailing ships, who used the products on their vessels. Petroleum-based goods eventually eliminated the more costly turpentining.

Twenty boardwalks ease the trail through swamps, where towering bald cypress, black gum, and sweet bay trees form a cooling canopy. Cypress knees, odd growths resembling a human knee, jut out of the water here and there, never developing foliage. In sunnier

Left: Banded water snakes are among the more common wildlife species that find the warm Florida climate to their liking. JOE MAC HUDSPETH
Right: The swollen trunks of cypress trees edge Trout Pond, in the Osceola National Forest. PHOTO COURTESY OF USDA FOREST SERVICE

sections, the sapphire-blue flower spikes of the pickerelweed are plentiful. Look closely along creek and swamp banks and you may sight another species that prefers sun—the alligator, descendant of the dinosaur.

Hunters favor Big Gum Swamp Wilderness, 13,660

formidable acres of hot, humid, thick vegetation without trails or roads, where a compass is a necessity.

This is the unexpected range of the Osceola—a groomed sandy beach to a wild primordial swamp, all within minutes of a bustling highway.

Apalachicola

N A T I O N A L   F O R E S T

There is no need to drive beyond the city limits of Florida's capital to enter the Southeast's largest national forest because the Apalachicola actually extends into Tallahassee, the only national forest to share ground with a state capital. The immense forest of longleaf, slash, and loblolly pines covers more than 560,000 acres in the Panhandle, forming the biggest, most consolidated block of public land east of the Rocky Mountains.

Despite its urban boundary, the Apalachicola, established in 1936, retains untamed pockets, particu-

larly in the swamps of Bradwell Bay Wilderness, named for a hunter lost in the vast thicket of titi or buckwheat tree (a bay here means a broad stretch of low land between hills). Visitors today have an advantage over poor Bradwell because the Florida National Scenic Trail passes through the wilderness. Even so, only the hardy are encouraged to enter, and they should prepare to get wet, because waist-deep water is not uncommon.

Water is a constant throughout the Apalachicola, providing recreation and benefiting wildlife and the

health of surrounding ecosystems. Watersheds of five rivers and one major stream send a steady flow to Apalachicola and Ochlockonee Bays to the south, which are famous for oysters and other seafood. The rivers themselves give anglers a good chance of success, along with 2,735 acres of lakes. Most of the eleven campgrounds adjoin water, and boat ramps are scattered throughout the forest, along with eight designated canoe trails. While no whitewater rapids exist on the Apalachicola or any of Florida's national forests, dense vegetation, alligators, and insects offer their own challenges. Canoeing is arguably the best way to see the most remote part of the forest, the Mud Swamp/New River Wilderness, a wetland densely covered by titi and slash pine.

Uninterrupted stands of longleaf pine make the Apalachicola the largest remaining refuge for the endangered red-cockaded woodpecker. The bird nests inside cavities it creates within living pine trees, with the longleaf its primary choice. Logging and development have eliminated all but mostly unsuitable islands of longleaf pine outside national forests, so the Forest Service pursues aggressive steps to protect the bird's habitat (see sidebar story).

Motorists pass through red-cockaded woodpecker territory on the Apalachee Savannas Scenic Byway, comprised of State Highway 65 and County Roads 12 and 379. The drive gives an overview of the Apalachicola's diversity of forests, swamps, and savannas, which are popular for their wildflowers. In bogs, the carnivorous pitcher plant is an interesting phenomenon as it attracts insects, then captures and digests them in rolled leaves.

Mountain bicycle enthusiasts can try their mettle on the challenging Munson Hills Bike Trail of roller-coaster dips and turns, while horseback riders will find a more docile route

Above left: The endangered red-cockaded woodpecker excavates its nests in living pine trees. Only seven inches long at maturity, the bird lives in colonies. C. C. LOCKWOOD

Left: Sundew plants digest insects to compensate for poor soils. GLENN VAN NIMWEGEN

PRESCRIBED BURNING

After years of watching Smokey Bear plead for everyone to fight forest fires, seeing a national forest deliberately set ablaze can be alarming. But prescribed or controlled burning serves many uses, from improving wildlife habitat to minimizing impact of lightning-induced fires.

Below left: Planned fires minimize wildfire risks and serve other uses.
PHOTO COURTESY OF USDA FOREST SERVICE - WILLIAM J. WEBER
Left: Wildflowers flourish in the nitrogen-rich soils after fires.
PHOTO COURTESY OF USDA FOREST SERVICE - WILLIAM J. WEBER

Foresters, for example, burn growth beneath longleaf pines because the endangered red-cockaded woodpecker will nest only in areas clear of thick midstory vegetation. The Apalachicola, because of its importance to the birds, has the largest prescribed fire program of all national forests, with nearly 57,000 acres burned in a single year. Scientists now look to the Apalachicola as a primary source of the woodpeckers to supplement declining populations in other forests in the South.

Managed burns also are significant because they minimize wild fire danger by eliminating such volatile fuels as fallen limbs. Without intentional burning, an unplanned blaze could spread uncontrollably within a national forest and beyond, endangering lives and property. Most prescribed burns, on the other hand, leave trees unharmed. Bark will blacken, but the crowns remain alive. Indeed, some trees, like the sand pine, require intense heat for seed germination.

Fire is also used to combat some tree diseases, to enrich soils, and to encourage growth of plants favored by deer and other species. Visitors may also see burning to prepare sites for planting tree seedlings, a common timber practice. In each of these instances, fires are started when temperature, humidity, and wind are most favorable for controlling the burn.

---

on the Vinzant Riding Trail through wooded roads and bays. Another tranquil setting, devised expressly for persons with disabilities, but open to everyone, is Trout Pond Recreation Area, which features the Discovery Trail of educational stops about the environment. Fishing is accessible on a shaded pier, and paved trails are provided to ensure even walking surfaces and easy wheelchair access.

At Leon Sinks Geological Area, six miles of hiking trails, boardwalks, and scenic overlooks offer views of five major sinkholes, or natural depressions, and other smaller sinks, all of them caused by subsurface collapse. Swimming and climbing on the banks of the sinks, some of which are more than 200 feet deep and filled with water, threatened the delicate environment and have been restricted.

There is also a place to review some of the Apalachicola's human history at Fort Gadsden State Historic Site overlooking the Apalachicola River. First used by the British in 1814, and ultimately by Confederate troops, the site has a free outdoor display detailing its violent past. 🌲

Ocala
NATIONAL FOREST DIRECTORY

POINTS OF INTEREST

Ocala National Forest Visitors center Good place to start exploring through free wildlife and historical displays. Maps, guides, brochures, local foods available, with profits invested in the forest. Volunteer Interpretive Association members answer questions and sponsor tours. 10863 E. Highway 40, Silver Springs, FL. 34488; (904) 625-7470

Pittman Visitor Center Smaller than Ocala center, but same resources. 45621 State Road 19, Altoona, FL. 32702; (904) 669-7495

Alexander Springs Recreation Area Provides sampling of Ocala's striking vegetation, from dry sand pine scrub to lush oak hammocks. Timucuan Indian Trail especially scenic and informative.

Fore Lake Nearly eight acres in size, with 250-foot, sandy beach. Swimming, fishing, boating (in small, non-gasoline powered craft), and camping.

WILDERNESS AREAS

Alexander Springs Creek Wilderness 7,941 acres, adjacent to the St. Johns River. Hardwood swamp and some sand pine scrub. Can be reached on Forest Service Road 552, going east from County Road 445, north of Umatilla.

Billie's Bay Wilderness 3,092 acres, predominantly hardwood swamp. West of Alexander Springs Creek Wilderness, just off State Road 19.

Juniper Prairie Wilderness 14,281 acres, dozens of ponds interspersed among tallgrass prairies and pine and oak forests. Contains about seven miles of the Florida National Scenic Trail. From Ocala, drive east on State Road 40 for about twenty-eight miles.

Little Lake George Wilderness 2,833 acres of pine and hardwood timber. Take State Road 40 east about twelve miles from Ocala. Then go north on County Road 314 about eighteen miles, then north on State Road 19 about nine miles, and east on Forest Service Road 77 for about one-third of a mile.

RECREATIONAL OPPORTUNITIES

Hiking and riding 219 miles of trails, including sixty-six miles of Florida National Scenic Trail (FNST) tracing the length of forest, with frequent access points. FNST passes eight recreation areas, sixty lakes and ponds. Shorter trails at Clearwater Lake, Lake Eaton, Alexander Springs, Juniper Springs, Buck Lake, Farles Lake, Hopkins Prairie, Lake Delancy, and Salt Springs.

The Ocala One-hundred Mile Horse Trail Divided into three sections on old logging roads. Flatwoods Trail a forty-mile loop through longleaf pine. Prairie Trail also forty miles and goes through grassy prairies and sand pine scrub. Baptist Lake Trail is a twenty-mile loop to Baptist Lake and back. Trailheads for all three off State Road 19, about two miles north of Altoona.

Camping 735 designated sites in eighteen areas. Camping with any motor vehicle or trailer is allowed only in designated sites. Tent camping is allowed throughout most of the forest, except for safety reasons during the general gun hunting season, usually from mid-Novemenber through early January.

Boating Eleven lakes open to boating, some restricted to non-gasoline powered boats only. Twenty boat ramps, half accessible only to four-wheel-drive vehicles.

Canoeing Widely popular, from seven-mile run at Alexander Springs to prairie lakes. Rentals available at Salt Springs, Juniper and Alexander Springs Recreation Areas. Heavy demand in peak summer season, so arrive early for rentals.

Swimming Restricted in some springs sections, but generally allowed throughout forest.

Scuba diving Permitted by certified divers with cards in specified areas only.

Hunting White-tailed deer favored. Also bobwhite quail, rabbit, squirrel, and dove. Florida Game and Fresh Water Fish Commission sets seasons, limits, and issues licenses.

Fishing Exceptional in twenty-three streams and 600 lakes. Largemouth bass, bluegill, speckled perch, redbreast, and catfish are plentiful.

Bird watching Climate and water attract many resident and migratory birds, including the scrub jay and endangered Southern bald eagle. Bird lists available at Visitor Centers.

Off-road vehicles No designated trails, but ORVs permitted unless posted signs state restrictions. Contact a district office for details.

ADMINISTRATIVE OFFICES

Forest Headquarters 325 John Knox Rd., Suite F-100 Tallahassee, FL 32303 (904) 942-9300.

Lake George Ranger District 17147 E. Highway 40, Silver Springs, FL 34488 (904) 625-2520.

Seminole Ranger District 40929 State Road 19, Umatilla, FL 32784 (904) 669-3153.

Osceola
NATIONAL FOREST DIRECTORY

POINTS OF INTEREST

Osceola District Ranger Office Contains interpretive display about turpentining and other historic and biological aspects of the forest. U. S. Highway 90, Olustee, FL.

Olustee Battlefield State Historic Site Free museum about decisive Civil War battle reenacted every February. Off U.S. 90, in town of Olustee.

WILDERNESS AREAS

Big Gum Swamp Wilderness 13,660 acres of cypress-gum swamps with a perimeter of pine flatwoods. No trails.

RECREATIONAL OPPORTUNITIES

Hiking Twenty-one miles of Florida National Scenic Trail through cypress swamps and pine forests. Short interpretive trail follows Olustee battlefield.

Camping Ocean Pond most developed campground with fifty shady sites, many overlooking water. Primitive camping at Hog Pen, also overlooking water, and in huntcamps maintained during hunting season. Dispersed camping permitted in most areas except during hunting seasons.

Canoeing and boating On Ocean Pond. Two fully developed boat ramps. A fishing pier for persons with disabilities is available at Olustee Beach.

Swimming and water skiing In Ocean Pond. Showers and changing rooms provided in day-use area at Olustee Beach.

Hunting White-tailed deer, wild turkey, feral hogs, quail, squirrel, raccoon, and waterfowl. Florida Game and Fresh Water Fish Commission sets seasons, limits, and issues licenses.

Bird watching Climate and water attract many resident and migratory birds, including the endangered red-cockaded woodpecker. Bird lists available at the district office.

Fishing In Ocean Pond for speckled perch, bass, and bluegill.

Off-road vehicles No designated areas, but permitted unless areas are marked restricted. ORV map available from district office.

ADMINISTRATIVE OFFICES

Forest Headquarters 325 John Knox Rd., Suite F-100, Tallahassee, FL 32303 (904) 942-9300

Osceola District US Highway 90, P.O. Box 70, Olustee, FL 32072 (904) 752-2577

Apalachicola
NATIONAL FOREST DIRECTORY

POINTS OF INTEREST

Leon Sinks Geologic Area Can be reached seven miles from Tallahassee by U.S. 319. A network of deep, water-filled and dry sinks, observation platforms, and trails with bridges through gum swamps.

Fort Gadsden State Historic Site Overlooks the Apalachicola River off Forest Service Road 129, six miles southwest of Sumatra. Seventy-eight acres with outdoor display about site's military use from 1814 through the Civil War.

WILDERNESS AREAS

Bradwell Bay Wilderness 24,600 acres of dense, remote swamp that contains hardwood and titi thickets, and small ponds mixed with scrubby pond pine. Usually wet.

Mud Swamp/New River Wilderness 8,090 acres with New River running through dense swamp covered with titi and slash pine.

RECREATIONAL AREAS

Hiking and riding More than 122 miles of trails, including sixty-six miles of Florida National Scenic

Trail, Munson Hills Bike Trail, Vinzant Riding Trail. Discovery National Recreation Trail designed for universal accessibility.

Camping Eleven campgrounds, open seasonally. Dispersed camping allowed in most of the forest.

Scenic Drive Apalachee Savannas Scenic Byway covers thirty-one miles along State Highway 65 and County Roads 12 and 379. An overview of forests, swamps, and savannas, noted for wildflowers. White paint bands denote nesting trees of endangered red-cockaded woodpeckers.

Boating and canoeing On 2,735 acres of lakes, five rivers and two major streams. Eight designated canoe runs.

Hunting White-tailed deer, turkey, squirrel, quail, fox, rabbit, opposum, bobcat, and dove. Limited waterfowl. Florida Game and Fresh Water Fish Commission sets seasons, limits, and issues licenses.

Fishing Excellent river, stream, and lake fishing throughout the forest.

Off-road vehicles Mostly on old logging roads. No specific trails, but permitted unless posted signs state restrictions.

ADMINISTRATIVE OFFICES

Forest Headquarters 325 John Knox Rd., Suite F-100, Tallahassee, FL 32303 (904) 942-9300

Wakulla Ranger District US Highway 319, Route 6, Box 7860, Crawfordville, FL 32327 (904) 926-3561

Apalachicola District, State Highway 20, P.O. Box 579, Bristol, FL 32321 (904) 643-2282

A raccoon prepares for a quick escape. FRED WHITEHEAD

The Caribbean National Forest is the only tropical rain forest in the national forest system. Bromeliads and giant ferns are typical of the lush vegetation. THOMAS R. FLETCHER

Caribbean

N A T I O N A L   F O R E S T

Curtains of rain

The emerald green Puerto Rican parrot is an appropriate symbol for the Caribbean National Forest, the bird's only known home. Fewer than forty of these colorful creatures survive in the wild from a former island-wide population approaching one million. The parrot is ranked among the most endangered species in the world, with loss of habitat because of human encroachment the main cause for its precarious state.

As the only tropical rain forest among the United States national forests, the importance of the small Puerto Rican enclave of 28,000 acres is much bigger than its size might suggest. The United Nations has recognized this forest's unique ecosystem and designated it a Biosphere Reserve. The Caribbean National Forest, unlike most other rain forests, is managed for various uses, including recreation. Island residents flock to the forest's coolness, especially on summer weekends and holidays, to enjoy its many waterfalls and streams. And besides harboring many rare species, the forest contains the fifty-three-year-old International Institute of Tropical Forestry, where representatives from other tropical nations learn how to wisely use their natural resources. Biologists also share successful strategies for saving jeopardized wildlife, from operating breeding programs to reducing threats from predators.

The opportunity for educating the general public is also significant. About one million visitors annually, many of them European and American cruise ship passengers, visit the forest, which is about an hour's drive from the busy ports of San Juan. El Portal del Yunque Tropical Forest Center, to open in late 1995, will further awareness about this and other tropical rain forests through a combined visitor center, environmental education facility, and training complex for forest managers. Programs to help teachers instruct school children about sound environmental practices will be an important part of the center. Like the Puerto Rican parrot, tropical rain forests are critically endangered. People destroy millions of acres of rain forests every year, and if the trend continues at current rates, experts estimate all rain forests could be gone by the turn of the century. Approximately forty percent of all the world's vegetation grows in tropical rain forests, and as they disappear, unknown benefits the plants and trees may have for human life also vanish. Consequences for air quality and climate, scientists warn, could be disastrous for everyone, apart from the irreplaceable loss of wildlife.

El Yunque is what Puerto Ricans call the forest, as well as one peak in the Sierra de Luquillo Mountains, which is often shrouded in misty clouds. Taino Indians, who once inhabited the island, believed that gods lived on the cloudy peaks, which they gave a name meaning "white or sacred lands." Fifteenth-century Spanish explorers mistakenly translated the Taino term to "Yunque," or "anvil."

Petroglyphs etched in some of the forest's rocks are one of several reminders of the Indians, whose influence is also evident in local foods, language, and place names. The impact of Spanish colonizers is also strong and continues to be felt in modern-day Puerto Rico. Maps and brochures are written in both Spanish and English and all forest visitor representatives are bilingual. In fact, it was King Alfonso XII of Spain who set aside about half of the Caribbean National Forest in 1876, making it one of the oldest forest reserves in the western hemisphere. His foresight spared El Yunque from massive deforestation that reduced the number of trees by ninety percent elsewhere on this island. Many trees were cut to clear the way for coffee and sugar cane plantations, just as many tropical forests today are leveled for crop production and wood. In Puerto Rico, however, replanting and natural regeneration have replaced about a third of the lost trees. Rain is almost a constant factor in parts of the forest, especially on high summits, where up to 240 inches can fall in a year at elevations of 3,500 feet. The headwaters of six major rivers rise in the forest, providing a vital water source for agricultural and domestic uses. Overall, El Yunque gets an average yearly rainfall of 120 inches or more than 100 billion gallons. Rain gear is always prudent, especially for hikers and campers. But showers often pass swiftly, and shelters are spaced

Left: *The Puerto Rican land snail thrives in the heavy rainfall of El Yunque.* THOMAS R. FLETCHER
Right: *Some 200 fern varieties grow in the forest, a botanist's paradise.* THOMAS R. FLETCHER

along some trails for waiting out the downpours.

Many visitors, however, never stray far from Highway 191, the forest's main road, which passes by many of its most popular attractions, including Sierra Palm Visitor Information Center, where exhibits describe the forest's natural history, and maps and other information are available. Campers can obtain free permits at the center, and at the District Office at the northern entrance of the forest, although requesting permits in advance by writing is advisable. No overnight facilities exist in the forest, but dispersed camping is allowed. While it's unlikely anyone will be turned away, the number of campers is controlled to minimize impact.

Even from the road, scarlet petals of hibiscus flowers and a profusion of some of the forest's more than eighty orchid varieties are visible as they mix with the myriad shades of green of other plants and trees. The web of giant ferns, leaves, and vines is so thick that seeing beyond only a few feet can be difficult in places. More than 200 fern species thrive in the moist climate. Some might mistakenly assume that this jungle-like world is how the entire forest looks, but there are actually four distinct ecological zones. The lowest level, the Tabonuco forest, is found below 2,000 feet, and is named for the straight and tall tabonuco trees, which are among 225 native tree species in the forest, including twenty-three that grow nowhere else in the world. The tabonuco zone is the only true rain forest in El Yunque.

In the next zone, the Palo Colorado forest at 2,000 feet, lives the Puerto Rican parrot, which nests in cavities of the palo colorado trees. This area is characterized by valleys and gentle slopes. The precarious state of the endangered bird was made even more difficult by Hurricane Hugo, which roared out of the Atlantic Ocean in 1989 into El Yunque. The storm caused heavy damage and closed the forest for five months. Many trees were lost and soils were left vulnerable to immense landslides. Nearly $3 million in repairs have been made, and because of that work—and natural regeneration—much of the damage is now indiscernible to casual observers. Half of the wild Puerto Rican parrots, however, perished. An aviary in El Yunque, operated by the Forest Service with the U.S. Fish and Wildlife Service, was not harmed, however, and its captive parrot population of approximately seventy birds is used to supplement the numbers of wild birds. Some success is also coming from artificial nests installed to compensate for the limited number of natural nest trees and to enhance the bird's breeding capacity.

The Sierra Palm forest, the third zone, has much steeper terrain above 2,000 feet, while the final zone, the Dwarf, or Cloud forest, occupies the highest elevations above 2,500 feet. As its name implies, this region is marked by trees with stunted growth. Among the various frogs or coquí found in the highest forest is the Burrow Coquí. The Dwarf forest is the frog's only

Above: Twenty-seven miles of trail explore El Yunque, paths that are often slippery and steep. PHOTO COURTESY OF USDA FOREST SERVICE

Above right: A United Nations Biosphere Reserve, the forest is an important model for conservation and a site of international study. THOMAS R. FLETCHER

Below right: Guides speak both English and Spanish and conduct frequent tours for visitors who number more than one million annually. PHOTO COURTESY OF USDA FOREST SERVICE

known habitat, as it is for the Elfin Woods Warbler, a bird discovered in 1971 as a species new to science.

Twenty-seven miles of trails allow close observation of El Yunque's mysteries. The Big Tree Trail, which takes about an hour to walk round-trip, is among the most popular hikes and travels down through the Tabonuco forest to La Mina Falls, where hikers sometimes refresh themselves with a dunking in the natural pool at the base of the falls. Two other trails, the

Caimitillo and Baño de Oro, wind through sections favored by the Puerto Rican parrot, although the likelihood of spotting one is slim.

Pathways are often slippery and can be quite steep. Among the most challenging is the Tradewinds National Recreation Trail, a four-mile course through all four vegetation zones, including the higher elevations where easterly tradewinds offer agreeable breezes after a strenuous climb. The El Toro Trail is also rugged and rises to the top of a mountain by the same name, which is the highest peak in the forest at 3,533 feet. Careful stepping along narrow ridges is required. Still, the view from the mountain, assuming a lucky break in the habitual cloud cover, is spectacular. A good panorama is also found with considerably less effort by climbing the Yokahu lookout tower, which dates from the 1960s. The tower is only a short walk from Highway 191 and gives an uninterrupted 360-degree view. Another more strenuous climb, the El Yunque Trail, leads to the top of El Yunque Mountain, where an observation deck built by the Civilian Conservation Corps in the 1930s still stands. Communications antennas are found at two locations on these higher elevations in the forest, which are important for both public and military communications throughout the

Caribbean. Telephone service also depends on the forest's microwave repeater site. Altogether, nearly 200 separate communications functions depend on equipment located in El Yunque.

No hunting is allowed in the forest. Recreation, for most islanders who visit, especially in the hotter summer months, revolves around the many natural water features. Picnic shelters and facilities are provided in three separate areas, but picnicking is popular in other parts of the forest as well, along with wildlife and plant study.

Apart from the Puerto Rican parrot, the forest, like other places in the Caribbean and Latin America, is important to neotropical songbirds who winter here and spend the rest of the year in North America. Half of the forest's sixty-eight bird species migrate and lately their numbers appear to be dwindling, probably because of habitat loss, both in the tropics and northern climates. Forest managers are promoting cooperation to spread awareness of the birds' plight and steps to prevent further losses.

Botanists throughout the world are attracted to El Yunque for its rich array of vegetation, which includes the Baño de Oro Research Natural Area. These 2,172 acres are set aside to preserve virgin forest, which has

The beautiful and endangered Puerto Rican parrot is found exclusively within the Caribbean National Forest. PHOTO COURTESY OF USDA FOREST SERVICE

all but disappeared from the rest of the island. Other parts of El Yunque, which has yet another name, Luquillo Experimental Forest, are used for research of both natural and plantation forest types, such as mahogany, suitable in tropical climates. Knowledge gained is once again shared with others in the accelerating leadership role the Caribbean National Forest plays in averting the end of tropical rain forests. ♣

Visitors to Mount Britton observation tower may have to wait for a break in the clouds to enjoy the view, but the delay is rewarded with spectacular sights. PHOTO COURTESY OF USDA FOREST SERVICE

Caribbean
NATIONAL FOREST DIRECTORY

POINTS OF INTEREST

Sierra Palm Visitor Information Center Open daily, has interpretive displays, maps, and other information about the forest. Several trailheads are located nearby, along with picnic areas.

WILDERNESS AREAS

None in the forest yet, but several areas are under consideration.

RECREATIONAL OPPORTUNITIES

Hiking Twenty-seven miles of trails. Some sections are extremely rugged and slippery because of frequent rainfall; others are moderately difficult.

Camping No facilities but dispersed camping is allowed. Free permits required.

Scenic Drives Highway 191 passes many of the forest's attractions, including scenic waterfalls. Access from the north side only—highway closed at KM 13.5

Hunting Prohibited.

Picnicking Popular in three designated areas and many additional locations.

Off-Road Vehicles Prohibited.

Guided Tours Offered by Forest Service personnel. Call the District Office about two weeks in advance to make a reservation.

ADMINISTRATIVE OFFICES

Forest Headquarters P. O. Box 25000, Rio Piedras, Puerto Rico 00928-2500 (809) 766-5335. Located at the Jardín Botánico on the University of Puerto Rico campus in Rio Piedras, a suburb of San Juan.

El Yunque Ranger District P. O. Box B, Palmer, Puerto Rico 00721 (809) 887-2875. Located just off Highway 191 at km 4.3 at the northern entrance to the forest.

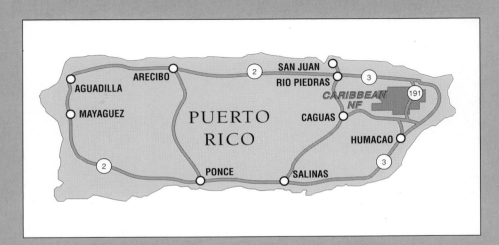

Cheaha Mountain is the highest summit in Alabama at 2,407 feet. A scenic drive leads through Talladega National Forest to the mountain top where there is a state park. The view from the crest takes in miles of forests and the distant city of Anniston. TOM TILL

Alabama

Bankhead • Talladega • Tuskegee • Conecuh

Lands of varied beauty

Mountains in Alabama? Many may be surprised to learn that this Deep South state known for farms actually has peaks over 2,000 feet tall, many of them within national forests. Elevations, in fact, vary significantly in Alabama's four forests, dropping to 100 feet in the Coastal Plain.

High overlooks, rolling hills, and tree-studded flat lands are among the contrasting terrains in the forests. Hikers enjoy an extensive network of trails, with some of the pathways crisscrossing two designated wildernesses. There are also quiet drives with far-reaching scenic views and a special walk-in area designed for seeing wildlife. Boaters and water skiers can enjoy a large, clean lake, which has enough quiet coves to satisfy anglers as well. Besides the many recreational opportunities, the forests provide habitats for some 900 species of birds, fish, and animals, including threatened, endangered, and sensitive species like the gopher tortoise and flattened musk turtle.

Covering some 658,755 acres, the forests generate revenue through leasing for mineral rights and cattle grazing, but mostly through timber sales, with nearly 75 million board feet cut annually, largely yellow pines. There is also an active oil well on the Conecuh National Forest in the southern portion of the state, with several more wells expected. The forests additionally are important watersheds for seven municipalities serving 350,000 people.

Bankhead

N A T I O N A L   F O R E S T

Few outdoor dining spots could be more arresting than the picnic ground overlooking the Sipsey River in the Bankhead National Forest in northern Alabama. Statuesque old poplars, sycamores, and beeches spread their limbs in a giant umbrella, shading tables spaced well apart along a bending path. Past the tables, the trail follows the base of a succession of tall rock bluffs vividly decorated with lichens and mosses. Thousands of crevices support other vegetation, including lush ferns, while rock ledges and overhangs invite closer scrutiny and climbing.

The bluffs wrap around coves cooler and moister than the surrounding countryside. But even here, effects of a dry season are evident. A waterfall, dropping more than fifty feet over rock tiers, has dwindled to a trickle, and the Sipsey River, Alabama's only wild and scenic waterway, has shrunk to a narrow lazy stream.

Nearby, however, within the Sipsey Wilderness, the river is still deep enough to form a pool where a group of friends has gathered to enjoy leaping from big boulders into the water. Their laughter punctuates the stillness of the pristine wilderness, where more old-growth trees are found. This oasis has drawn human beings for as long as 8,000 years, beginning with prehistoric Indians, who left many signs of their existence in the Bankhead, which occupies 180,054 acres. Later Alabama residents, sympathetic to the Union, hid among the bluffs from Confederate Rebels.

Today, visitors come with many different expectations. Some launch canoes in the Sipsey River, usually navigable from November through May. There is one set of fairly tame rapids on this enjoyable journey through dramatic corridors of sandstone bluffs, but only the lower sections near Lake Lewis Smith are usually deep enough for floating in summer.

Year-round, hikers enter the Sipsey Wilderness, where a trail weaves next to the river, then climbs into the woods, and edges back to the river again. More rock bluffs create sheltered coves that are welcome in warmer months, but hikers should be alert for hornets and yellow jackets, which can be territorial and menacing. In spots, the path is ill-defined and there are feeder creeks to cross with unreliable stepping stones. Yet these challenges contribute to the wilderness experience, further heightened by chance sightings of deer, fox, and other wildlife, and myriad wildflowers. Yellow coreopsis, purple spiderworts, and red cardinal flowers thrive near the walkways.

Equestrians will find thirty miles of trails and a primitive campground with space for horses at Owl Creek, near Brushy Lake Recreation Area, where there is more camping, including trailer sites. Fishing is temporarily prohibited in the thirty-three-acre lake, which was emptied of all water by vandals. Water levels

The Sipsey Wild and Scenic River courses through the Bankhead National Forest. Portions flowing through the Sipsey Wilderness are popular for swimming, while tributaries and creeks tumble over rock falls nearby. TOM TILL

SMALL BUT DEADLY

One of the most destructive pests in the South, the southern pine beetle, is no bigger than a grain of rice. Adults bore inside pines to carve S-shaped egg galleries. When the eggs hatch, the larvae feed voraciously on the trees, strangling them by cutting off moisture and nutrients. Depending upon their numbers, they can quickly kill either a few trees or destroy hundreds of acres.

Damaged pines are cut to prevent spreading the infestation. In Alabama in 1991, about 19.4 million board feet of timber struck by the beetle was salvaged, enough wood to build 1,662 new houses. Small scattered outbreaks are sometimes dealt with by cutting and leaving trees, especially in hard-to-reach areas. Some of these pines are eventually burned or salvaged.

Voracious pine beetle larvae destroy acres of Southern forests. C.C. LOCKWOOD

have returned to normal, but restocked fish need time to grow—reopening is anticipated in August of 1993. A few miles south stands Natural Bridge, a sandstone arch millions of years old where observation platforms offer views from above and below. Picnic tables are provided close by.

Among the most popular of all activities in the forest is boating on Lake Lewis Smith. This 2,100-acre lake comes alive in summer with motorboats churning up the waters. Water skiers delight in leaping wakes and performing other feats. But the lake is big enough to accommodate a variety of interests. Anglers have many quiet coves to choose from and swimmers can safely enjoy the clean water and a sandy beach near Clear Creek Recreation Area. This is the newest and largest campground in the forest, with water and electrical hookups at every site. A bicycle and hiking trail curves along the shore and there is a nature trail loop nearby that showcases more of the cliffs and waterfalls that help make the Bankhead appealing.

Talladega

N A T I O N A L   F O R E S T

The search for the highest ground in Alabama ends in the Talladega National Forest, where the southernmost thrust of the Appalachian Mountains begins in the northeast part of the state. Within the Talladega's 384,591 acres stands the highest peak in Alabama, Cheaha Mountain, at 2,407 feet. Cheaha, in fact, is an Indian word meaning "high," a description also suitable for the nearby Cheaha Wilderness where more than 1,000 acres stand above 2,000 feet.

While these mountains are not as steep as most others in the sprawling Appalachian range, they can still be rugged. Trees stunted from harsh weather cling to summits where thin soils expose quartz-streaked rocks. Hiking trails within the Cheaha Wilderness are rocky and quite steep in places. The most traveled is a section of the Pinhoti National Recreation Trail, which traces through the wilderness for about seven miles and continues through other forest lands for a total of about eighty miles. Plans call for the path to be extended to Georgia and to merge with the Appalachian Trail.

A much easier hike leads from a parking area to an overlook atop Cheaha Mountain with a good view of the valley below. Purple spikes of blazing star flowers color the ground near the edge of the lookout point and the sky takes on a similar shade as the sun sets. Twilight rouses hundreds of bats from their resting places in the mountain's crags. They sweep furiously past the overlook with sharp calls, then dart through the air. White-tailed deer are also most likely to be visible in the same hours as they browse in the woods of the state park that occupies the mountaintop. Campsites, a hotel and restaurant, group lodge, and store are located in the Cheaha State Park, which also has a swimming pool and wildflower garden. The Civilian Conservation Corps erected some of the buildings in the 1930s.

The Talladega Scenic Drive makes the mountain ascent enjoyable in itself, with several overlooks along the way. The byway, about twenty miles long, is accessible from Interstate 20, the busy thoroughfare connecting Birmingham with Atlanta. The difference between the two roadways is stark and immediate: while the highway roars around the clock with trucks and cars, it's possible to travel stretches of the byway without meeting any traffic. Even the scenic route, however, can bustle in fall, when the oaks, maples, hickories, and persimmons display their brightest hues.

Seeing the autumn leaves is as favorite a pastime here as it is in many of the northern Appalachians. But the Talladega's dogwoods and redbuds make the forest equally appealing in spring, although crowds are fewer.

The Pinhoti Trail parallels the byway before continuing through the Cheaha Wilderness and beyond. Pinhoti is a combination of Creek Indian words—"pinwa," meaning "turkey," and "huti" or "home." The forest is indeed home to many wild turkey, and hikers may chance upon them. The startled birds may race on foot out of sight or flap briefly into the air before disappearing. Red-tailed hawks, eastern bluebirds, and many other songbirds also inhabit the forest. The trail travels to many of the best recreation sites in this stretch of the Talladega and to a number of its most visually appealing spots. Waterfalls, crystal clear streams, and frequent vistas line the way, as well as places of historical interest. The Shoal Creek Church, for example, was built in the late 1800s and is one of only six hand-hewn churches left in Alabama.

Not far from Cheaha Mountain is Lake Chinnabee Recreation Area on Forest Service Road 646, where a twenty-acre lake and small campground are tucked into a pastoral valley. Fishing is excellent and an easy two-mile trail encircles the lakeshore. There is also the Chinnabee Silent Trail, connecting the campground with Cheaha Wilderness. Boy Scouts from the Alabama School for the Deaf blazed the Chinnabee path, which is considered fairly strenuous in sections of its six miles.

The recreation area is one of several pleasant campgrounds in the Talladega, which has most of its recreation facilities in northeastern Alabama. Part of the forest, however, is farther west and south, separated from the rest by private lands and another highway, Interstate 65. This southern region falls within the Oakmulgee Ranger District where there is one campground with seventy-seven sites in the Payne Lake Recreation Area. The lake covers 110 acres and is popular for fishing, with bluegill, crappie, redear sunfish, and largemouth bass the favored quarries.

The trumpet-shaped flowers of Virginia bluebells open from pink buds in early spring. Bluebells prefer moist woods, and Alabama marks the southern border of their range. J. C. LEACOCK

Tuskegee · Conecuh

For watching wildlife outdoors, there is probably no better place in Alabama than the Tsinia Wildlife Viewing Area. Situated in the Tuskegee National Forest near Montgomery, the enclave includes 125 acres off limits to hunting. Tsinia means "peeping" or "viewing" in the Creek Indian tongue, and forest managers have worked to ensure that visitors will have plenty to see. Edible vegetation appealing to many species has been planted and effectively attract deer, turkey, rabbit, quail, and other creatures.

Visitors can observe them from a trail accessible to the disabled, which includes a boardwalk over wetlands. Look for colorful wood ducks and great blue herons along the way. An observation blind is erected for birdwatching as well. In the opposite direction, the path leads to an observation tower and two beaver ponds where the corpulent residents may sometimes be spotted moving slowly through the water. Dead trees or snags are left to provide homes and roosts for various species. Among the birds frequenting the area is the rufous-sided towhee with reddish orange sides, spotted tail, and white belly.

Both of southern Alabama's forests, the 11,073-acre Tuskegee and 83,037-acre Conecuh, are home to many varieties of wildlife. And both also offer excellent long-distance hiking. In the Tuskegee, there is the Bartram Trail, honoring William Bartram, the Philadelphia naturalist who explored the territory in the late 1700s.

The trail rises and falls through rolling hill country and close to Choctafaula Creek. Many hikers travel the entire 8.5 miles in a day, while others walk only part way. Not far away, on U.S. Highway 29/80, is the Taska Recreation Area, a comfortable picnic ground in a pine forest, where there is also a replica of the house where Booker T. Washington was born. Washington rose from humble be-

Above: *Tsinia Wildlife Viewing Area in the Tuskegee National Forest offers 125 acres with easy trails and special observation points for enjoying birds, deer, and other wildlife. A boardwalk crosses over wetlands, providing a close-up view of waterfowl.* PHOTO COURTESY OF USDA FOREST SERVICE - JOY PATTY

Below: *Great Blue Herons are sometimes spotted at Tsinia Wildlife Viewing Area. Look for the dusky-blue birds wading in the shallows as they hunt for fish.* ADAM JONES

ginnings to become an important African American leader and head of the nearby Tuskegee Institute.

The Conecuh Trail is farther south in the flat Coastal Plain and extends through the Conecuh National Forest for twenty miles. Another group of Indians, the Muskogee, are credited for the name Conecuh, which means "land of cane." The trail passes several canebreaks, as well as groups of pond cypress with their intriguing swelled trunks and mysterious "knees." Hardwood bottomlands and stretches of longleaf pines are highlights along this popular hike. Few complete the entire length in less than two days, so dispersed camping is allowed along the way, except during hunting season from November through April. Day hikers are also common along the trail's three loop sections. The easy path features several bridges across streams and skirts a number of water sites favored for bass fishing, including Open Pond where there is a year-round campground. Hikers also pass Blue Springs, a large natural spring of clear, icy-blue water.

Fishing is particularly noteworthy in the forest, especially in Brooks Hines Lake where the hybrid striped bass are valued for their fight. Catfish weighing ten pounds have also been taken from the water. There are no fish, however, in Nellie Pond, designated as protected habitat for the dusky gopher frog, a sensitive species. ♣

Bankhead
NATIONAL FOREST DIRECTORY

POINTS OF INTEREST

Sipsey River Picnic Area Peaceful site near scenic rock bluffs. Take I-65 to U.S. 278 going west, then go north on Alabama Road 33. Turn left on Lawrence County Road 6, which crosses into Winston County and becomes Winston County Road 60.

Clear Creek Modern, full-facility campground on Lake Lewis Smith. From Jasper, take State Highway 195 to Manchester. Turn right on County Road 27 and the recreation area is a little more than eight miles away.

Houston Recreation Area offers three camping loops, a day use area for swimming and picnicking, and a boat launch on scenic Lewis Smith Lake. Take I-65 to U.S. Highway 278, at Cullman, go west past Addison. Continue west to County Road 63 and turn south. Go two miles and take FS Road 118 west to campground.

Brushy lake Recreation Area is nestled in a remote setting and offers a retreat from the bustle of everyday life. Go to Double Springs and take Alabama Highway 33 north to Forest Service Road 262. Follow this road for four miles to Brushy Lake.

Corinth Recreation Area is under renovation. It is to re-open in late 1994 or early 1995. Go to Double Springs and take U.S. Highway 278 east to County Road 57 and go south. This will take you to Corinth Recreation Area.

WILDERNESS AREAS

Sipsey 25,986 acres of rolling hill country, waterfalls, and sandstone cliffs. Located in northwestern portion of the forest, the wilderness has some old-growth trees.

RECREATIONAL OPPORTUNITIES

Hiking and Riding Miles of trails for hikers and horseback riders. Owl Creek Horse Camp is adjacent to nearly thirty miles of equestrian trails.

Camping and Picnicking Sites across the forest. Reservations accepted for some sites at Clear Creek. Primitive camping permitted throughout much of the forest, with permit from district ranger in fall deer hunting season.

Scenic Drives State Highway 33 runs north and south through the forest providing easy access to most attractions. The Forest Service offers a self-guided tour starting at the intersection of Highway 33 and Forest Service Road 208. Check with the Ranger Station for details.

Rafting, Canoeing, and Kayaking The Sipsey Wild and Scenic River is navigable in cooler months.

Fishing Redeye bass in streams, and crappie, bream, catfish, largemouth bass, and other fish in Lake Lewis Smith. Brushy Lake will reopen for fishing in August of 1993.

Hunting Deer, turkey, quail, rabbit, raccoon, and fox. State license required and special permits needed in the Black Warrior Wildlife Management Area.

Rifle Range Hurricane Creek Range is set up for targets at twenty-five, fifty, and 100 yards and also has archery sites.

Off-Road Vehicles A trail for all terrain vehicles is planned. Check with the Ranger Station for details.

ADMINISTRATIVE OFFICES

Forest Headquarters 1765 Highland Ave., Montgomery, AL 36107 (205) 832-4470

Bankhead Ranger District P. O. Box 278, South Main Street, Double Springs, AL 35553 (205) 489-5111

Talladega
NATIONAL FOREST DIRECTORY

POINTS OF INTEREST

Coleman Lake Recreation Area Popular campground and fishing spot north of Interstate 20, with access to Pinhoti National Recreation Trail.

Cheaha State Park Surrounded by the National Forest on Talladega Scenic Drive, the park includes Alabama's highest peak at 2,407 feet.

Payne Lake Recreation Area In west central part of the state near U.S. Highway 82. From west of Centreville, Alabama, take State Highway 5 south to State Highway 25, then go west for fifteen miles.

Lake Chinnabee Recreation Area located two miles south of Talladega County Road 42. This can be accessed from U.S. Highway 21, north of Talladega, or the Talladega Scenic Drive near Cheaha State Park.

WILDERNESS AREAS

Cheaha 7,490 acres of high country with many rock outcrops and scenic views. The Wilderness is near Interstate 20 connecting Birmingham and Atlanta.

RECREATIONAL OPPORTUNITIES

Hiking and Riding Excellent short and long hikes possible on the Pinhoti Trail.

Camping and Picnicking Various possibilities across the forest, including dispersed camping. During fall deer hunting season, permission required for dispersed camping.

Scenic Drives Talladega Scenic Byway is attractive year-round with far-reaching views. Near Interstate 20, take U.S. Highway 431.

Hunting Deer, turkey, racoon, rabbit, and fox. State license required. Check for special regulations and permit requirements in wildlife management areas.

Fishing Redeye bass in the streams. Numerous lakes stocked with varieties such as largemouth bass, bluegill, crappie, redear sunfish, bream, and catfish.

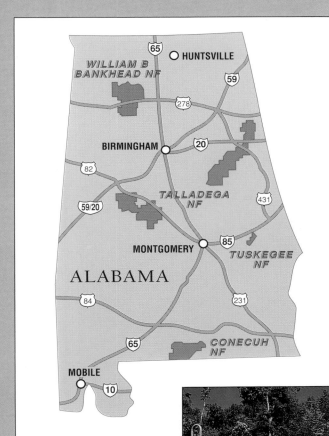

Clear Creek Recreation Area near Lake Lewis Smith is popular among campers.
PHOTO COURTESY OF USDA
FOREST SERVICE - TAMMY FREEMAN

Rafting, Canoeing, and Kayaking Some streams suitable.

ADMINISTRATIVE OFFICES

FOREST HEADQUARTERS 1765 Highland Ave., Montgomery, AL 36107 (205) 832-4470

SHOAL CREEK RANGER DISTRICT 450 Highway 46, Heflin, AL 36264 (205) 463-2272

TALLADEGA RANGER DISTRICT 1001 North Street, Talladega, AL 35160 (205) 362-2909

OAKMULGEE RANGER DISTRICT P. O. Box 67, Centreville, AL 35042 (205) 926-9765

Tuskegee • Conecuh
NATIONAL FOREST DIRECTORIES

POINTS OF INTEREST

Tsinia Wildlife Viewing Area Planted to attract animals and birds. Handicapped access on trails, viewing blind, and observation tower. Take I-85 north from Montgomery to exit 42 (Wire Road). Turn right on County Road 53 (Wire Road). Follow County Road 53 to Highway 29/80. Cross 29/80 to Forest Service Road 937. Tsinia parking lot is 200 yards down, on right.

Open Pond Campground and fishing in southern Alabama. Follow U.S. 29 southwest from Andalusia, then turn south onto State Road 137. Go left on County Road 24 for one-half mile and then right on Forest Service Road 336.

RECREATIONAL OPPORTUNITIES

Hiking and Riding Twenty-mile Conecuh Trail in the Conecuh National Forest and the 8.5-mile William Bartram Trail in the Tuskegee have easy grades through attractive landscapes.

Camping and Picnicking The Taska Recreation Area in the Tuskegee and Blue Pond in the Conecuh are popular picnic areas. Open Pond offers camping. Dispersed camping permitted through most of the forests, but permission required during fall hunting season.

Hunting Deer, turkey, racoon, squirrel, rabbit, and fox. State hunting license required. Special regulations apply in Blue Springs Wildlife Management Area.

Fishing Largemouth bass, spotted bass, bluegill, channel catfish, redear sunfish, longear sunfish, and other fish found at various places in the forests. Brooks Hines Lake, closed on Mondays and in December and January, known for big sport fish and feisty largemouth bass.

Shooting Free rifle ranges on both forests.

Off-Road Vehicles Prohibited unless signs indicate permission.

ADMINISTRATIVE OFFICES

Forest Headquarters 1765 Highland Avenue, Montgomery, AL 36107 (205) 832-4470

Tuskegee Ranger District Route 1, Box 269, Highway 186, 2 miles east of I-85, Tuskegee, AL 36083 (205) 727-2652

Conecuh Ranger District Route 5, Box 157, Andalusia, AL 36420 (205) 222-2555

The six national forests in Mississippi cover nearly one million acres of heavily wooded land. Ideal growing conditions help longleaf pines and other trees flourish, making the forests leading timber producers in the South.
C.C. LOCKWOOD

Mississippi

De Soto · Bienville
Tombigbee · Holly Springs · Delta · Homochitto

N A T I O N A L F O R E S T S

Deep south diversity

Mississippi's six national forests are an outdoor mosaic—from a dark creek curling through dense wilderness to a prairie rippling with tall grass. There is also an old-growth pine forest where visitors can wander amidst the mighty trees and see jagged scars on the trunks from long-ago lightning strikes. And there is a thriving hardwood forest in the delta region where every winter parts of the woodlands are intentionally flooded. This compensates for the loss of wetland habitat caused by levees built to control the Mississippi River's rampages, and , while the temporary inundation causes no harm to the dormant trees, it creates a welcome resting place for migrating waterfowl.

The forests also shelter a wealth of natural resources. Fertile soils and long growing seasons make Mississippi forests the top timber producers in South, with 223 million board feet harvested a year, while rich oil and gas reserves rank the forests high among revenue producers in those categories. Spread for more than one million acres across the state, the forests are within easy reach for many Mississippians, and provide opportunities for year-round recreational activities.

De Soto

Floating the waters of Black Creek beneath gracefully arching trees may be one of the best ways to appreciate the De Soto National Forest in southeastern Mississippi. Tannic acid from decaying vegetation gives Black Creek its name and dark tint, while magnolias and wild azaleas on the bluffs add their own colors. The languid current and banks never far apart allow close observation of the surrounding forest. Wide, white sandbars along the shores are popular for camping and picnicking, and with mostly unobstructed passage for forty miles the journey is an extended immersion in an unspoiled setting.

The De Soto, established in 1935, is named for Spanish explorer Hernando De Soto, who searched the South for gold in the sixteenth century. The forest, Mississippi's largest, is divided into two parts, totaling just over a half-million acres. The southern boundary is less than ten miles from Interstate 10 and the popu-lous Biloxi-Gulfport region.

Much of the forest is easily accessible from U.S. Highway 49, traveling north from Gulfport. Big Biloxi Campground, for instance, is close to the highway along Big Biloxi River. Continuing north, the highway passes rows of stately live oaks marking the entrance to Tuxachanie National Recreation Trail. The twenty-two mile hiking trail begins in the path of an old logging railroad built by Irish laborers using little more than simple hand tools. Remnants of the bridges, built around the turn of the century, can still be seen in streams along the trail.

Airey Lake, a small, three-acre lake, is also along the hiker's way. Like most forest lakes, this one supports many fish such as bass and bream. Past the lake, the trail climbs slight ridges enveloped in trees and shrubs, including gallberry, dogwood, and yaupon. Leaves of the evergreen yaupon contain caffeine and

were brewed by Native Americans into a hot beverage.

The trail also dips by swamps and grassy savannahs. Titi, an evergreen with leathery leaves, is prevalent, and the white blossoms in spring are irresistible to bees. Delicate wild orchids also flower near the path, as well as insect-eating pitcher plants. The trail ends at what was once the site of a World War II prison camp for German soldiers. Today, the site provides a peaceful pine setting and a primitive campground overlooking a small lake.

Farther north on U.S. 49 is Big Creek Landing, where trips frequently begin on Black Creek, designated a wild and scenic river. The landing is also a starting point for the Black Creek National Recreation Trail, which follows near the waterway for forty miles. This and other landings provide restrooms, picnic tables, and drinking water, but hikers must carry their own water on the trail. Eventually the trail leads into Black Creek Wilderness where prehistoric people trod the same ground and hunted among the sweetgums, poplars, and oaks. More than ninety footbridges help trail hikers pass over the many streams and soggy low ground.

The W. W. Ashe Nursery is also just off Highway 49 and visitors are welcome to see the only national forest nursery in the Southeast. The operation supplies superior tree seedlings for national forests throughout the South, and since 1936 has produced more than one billion young trees.

Another hiking trail explores part of the De Soto's other wilderness located on the east side of MS Highway 57. While relatively small at only 960 acres, Leaf Wilderness is an interesting conglomeration of sloughs, oxbow lakes, and uplands. Not far from the trail grows the largest oak for miles around, a water oak perhaps more than 150 years old.

The De Soto's second segment is north of Hattiesburg and offers a chance to learn about forestry practices through the Gavin Auto Tour, which loops around twelve miles of forest roads, with interpretive signs along the way. One stop shows how a stand of managed trees has fared compared with another area left largely untouched: the unmanaged trees are smaller and often diseased, compared to the bigger and healthier tended trees.

In the same vicinity, Turkey Fork Campground appeals to both fans of placid fishing lakes and those interested in power boats. Water skiing is permitted on 175 acres of a 240-acre lake, but only from noon to sunset, four days a week, and on Federal holidays.

Left: Irish laborers helped build the logging railroad, now the popular Tuxachanie National Recreation Trail, early in the nineteenth century.
PHOTO COURTESY OF USDA
FOREST SERVICE
Right: W. W. Ashe Nursery provides seedlings for many southern national forests.
PHOTO COURTESY OF USDA
FOREST SERVICE

Bienville · Tombigbee · Holly Springs

The giant trees at Bienville Pines Scenic Area are a revelation to anyone accustomed to pines the size of fat telephone poles typically grown across the Southeast. Some of the Mississippi trees are so big that even two adults can't reach all the way around their trunks. These titans, some 200 years old, are some of the last surviving old-growth trees in the state. Indeed, this 180-acre preserve is the largest tract of virgin pines left in the entire Southeast.

In the early 1900s when most Mississippi forests were logged, the loblolly and shortleaf pines here were left undisturbed. Today, visitors can enjoy this protected enclave along the Bienville Pines Trail.

The ancient pines are part of the Bienville National Forest, with 178,000 acres in the state's center, near Jackson. Within the forest, established in 1935, there is another protected sector where a different type of vegetation is important. Called the Harrell Prairie Hill Botanical Area, the area is reminiscent of the rural Midwest. Alkaline soils in the 150-acre preserve encourage growth of grasses and other plants entirely different from surrounding woodlands. This nearly

extinct plant community classified as Jackson Prairie was once found across Alabama and eastern Mississippi. But farmers plowed under the prairies and the lost species never returned. Scientists study this rare remnant and other nearby grass islands for clues about the sensitive plants and associated animals.

The Bienville is named for a French-Canadian soldier and colonist, Jean Baptiste Bienville, who founded Natchez, New Orleans, and Mobile. Besides its regions of botanical importance, the forest has many other attractions. The Shockaloe Horse Trail is a National Recreation Trail twenty-three miles long and challenges runners as well as horseback riders in some segments. There are also two campgrounds next to serene lakes. Marathon Lake Recreation Area is on the grounds of an old logging camp and has thirty-five shady campsites, while Shongelo Recreation Area has a smaller lake and four campsites. Both areas, easily accessible from Interstate 20, are only ninety minutes from Jackson.

Lakes are also prominent in Mississippi's northeastern forests—the Tombigbee, established in 1959, and Holly Springs, founded in 1935. Much of the land in these forests was formerly abandoned farms with eroding soils. Lakes were built to help repair the damage. An added benefit is the excellent fishing found in the warm waters. Choctaw Lake Recreation Area offers campsites, picnicking, and a fishing pier, all of which are accessible to the physically disabled. And Davis Lake, near Tupelo, in the Tombigbee, is especially popular among boating campers. Visitors often spend the day enjoying the water, then moor their boats by the shoreline campground at night.

Davis Lake is close to the Natchez Trace Parkway, a scenic and historic route travelling the length of Mississippi en route to Nashville, Tennessee. The parkway is a limited-access highway with wide shoulders and informative

The Shockaloe National Recreation Horse Trail explores deep woods and open spaces. PHOTO COURTESY OF USDA FOREST SERVICE

turnouts highlighting local history and geology, from sandy lowlands to rolling hills. Near Davis Lake, the Natchez Trace becomes a Forest Service Scenic Byway for fourteen miles. An offshoot, Davis Lake Road, passes by Owl Creek Mounds, where there are two prehistoric Native American burial and ceremonial mounds on Forest Service land, built sometime between A.D. 1000 and 1600. Originally there were three other mounds, all positioned around a central plaza. Two of the mounds still exist, though on privately owned land.

Nearby lies Witch Dance Horse Trail. According to legend, witches danced on the ground and the grass shriveled and died wherever their feet touched. Horses on the fifteen-mile loop splash through small streams and stir up wildlife, including deer, coyote, rabbits, and hawks.

Holly Springs is farthest north among the forests, not far from Tennessee. Its biggest recreation site is Chewalla Lake, which takes its name from the Choctaw Indian word for "supreme being." Like Owl Creek Mounds, this was once a special place for Native Americans, who built a ceremonial mound where the 260-acre lake now stands. A small mound is reconstructed on the lakeshore near a wooden overlook with a good view of the lake.

Just one hour from Memphis, Chewalla Lake offers developed campsites, picnic units, and accessible fishing piers. Originally built for flood retention, the lake is rarely overcrowded, even in summer. A sandy beach and lakeshore trail add to the recreational opportunities. The Forest Service is also developing a waterfowl refuge intended to attract mallards, pintails, and other ducks, as well as geese.

Delta · Homochitto

N A T I O N A L F O R E S T S

Much of the Delta National Forest in west-central Mississippi seems particularly untamed, a characteristic especially appealing to hunters, who don hip boots on cool mornings to wade into the forest's abundant wetlands. Many of the hunters, as well as a sizable number of anglers attracted to the forest, travel the backcountry roads in four-wheel-drive vehicles and spend the night in primitive camp sites scattered throughout the woods.

But even those who don't hunt or fish enjoy the unspoiled nature of the surroundings. The Delta is the only bottomland hardwood forest in the National Forest System. Bald cypress, tupelo gum, water oaks, and swamp maples are dominant. Flooding is part of the nature of the delta, a broad expanse of flat land backing up to the Mississippi River, literally

"the father of all waters" to early Native Americans.

The Delta National Forest was established in 1961, but managed by the Forest Service since 1935. The forest's vast, often soggy bottomlands are bordered in some places and crossed in others by the Big Sun-

Largemouth bass are among the most sought-after game fish in the US, and may be found in the lakes of the Bienville, DeSoto, Delta, Holly Springs, and Tombigbee national forests in Mississippi. PHOTO COURTESY OF USDA FOREST SERVICE

flower, Little Sunflower, and Yazoo Rivers.

Located on the migratory Mississippi flyway, the forest of about 60,000 acres is frequented by a multitude of bird species. Among the more distinctive to watch are the kingfishers diving headfirst into the rivers. Their long beaks are poised like sharp spears as they plunge after fish. Great blue herons are also commonly seen, high stepping near the water edges. A popular recreation area is Blue Lake, where camping and boating are available without charge.

The 187,195-acre Homochitto is near Natchez in southwest Mississippi. Rich soils, nourished with plentiful rains and sunshine, help make the Homochitto one of the foremost timber-producing southern forests. The Homochitto is also endowed with oil and natural gas deposits and plentiful wildlife.

Swimmers enjoy the clean waters of Clear Springs, a lake fed by natural springs surrounded by pines and hardwoods. A beach and bathhouse are popular for both daytime visitors and campers. A short trail circles the lake and there is another 10.5-mile loop trail nearby. ♣

De Soto
NATIONAL FOREST DIRECTORY

POINTS OF INTEREST

Big Biloxi A seventeen-unit campground on the banks of the Big Biloxi River. Take U.S. Highway 49 north from Gulfport. Go left or west on De Soto Park Road.

Big Creek Landing A launching site for float trips on Black Creek. The Black Creek Trail also starts here. Take U. S. Highway 49 north from Gulfport. Go left or west on Forest Service Road 334, then turn right on Forest Service Road 335 and right again on 335-E.

WILDERNESS AREAS

Black Creek 5,052 acres south of Hattiesburg, with dense woodlands and rolling hills. The Black Creek Trail crosses the wilderness.

Leaf 960 acres along Mississippi Highway 57, south and east of Hattiesburg. A 4.5-mile trail leads into this mostly low-lying forest.

RECREATIONAL OPPORTUNITIES

Hiking and Riding The forty-mile Black Creek National Recreation Trail and the twenty-two-mile Tuxachanie National Recreation Trail are the main hiking avenues. Shorter trails near major campgrounds. The two major equestrian areas are along the Big Foot and Longleaf Horse Trails.

Camping and Picnicking Developed campgrounds and primitive sites. Some sites may be reserved by calling 1-800-283-CAMP.

Rafting, Kayaking, and Canoeing Black Creek is a favorite for rafts, canoes, and jon boats. Mostly slow moving, the creek is usually navigable year-round, but can be dangerous in high water. Rentals available in Brooklyn, Mississippi.

Hunting Deer, turkey, quail, and other game. State license and regulations apply.

Fishing Bluegill, bass, bream, catfish, white perch, red bellies, shellcrackers, and carp in the lakes or streams. State license and regulations apply.

Off-Road Vehicles The sixty-nine-mile Bethel Trail accommodates all-terrain vehicles no wider than forty-eight inches primarily motorcycles and three- and four-wheelers. Located north of Gulfport.

ADMINISTRATIVE OFFICES

Forest Headquarters 100 W. Capitol St., Suite 1141, Jackson, MS 39269 (601) 965-4391

Biloxi Ranger District Route 1, Box 62, McHenry, MS 39561 (601) 928-5291

Black Creek Ranger District 1432 W. Border & Frontage Road, Box 248, Wiggins, MS 39577 (601) 928-4422

Chickasawhay Ranger District 418 S. Magnolia St., Box 426, Laurel, MS 39440 (601) 428-0594

Bienville • Tombigbee • Holly Springs
NATIONAL FORESTS DIRECTORY

POINTS OF INTEREST

Bienville Pines Scenic Area 180 acres of old-growth pine along a two-mile trail. From the town of Forest, between Jackson and Meridian on U.S. Highway 80, take State Highway 501 south for about one-half mile.

Harrell Prairie Hill Botanical Area Rare grassland supporting sensitive plants. From Forest, Mississippi, take State Highway 501 south one mile to Forest Road 518 and go two miles east.

Owl Creek Mounds Two mounds dated to the prehistoric Mississippian period. The mounds are near the Davis Lake Campground. From the Natchez Trace Parkway south of Tupelo, take Davis Lake Road and travel west three miles.

RECREATIONAL OPPORTUNITIES

Hiking and Riding Both short and longer hiking trails available, especially close to major recreation areas. The twenty-three-mile Shockaloe Horse Trail on the Bienville National Forest is a national recreation trail. The eighteen-mile Witch Dance Horse Trail starts at the Natchez Trace Parkway near Davis Lake.

Camping and Picnicking Numerous places for both. The Choctaw Lake Campground near Louisville on the eastern side of the state offers a number of activities and is near the Noxubee National Wildlife Refuge.

Scenic Drives The Natchez Trace Scenic Byway is a fourteen-mile scenic route that includes the Natchez Trace Parkway and a spur road, County Road 903, to Davis Lake. The route travels rolling hills and passes Owl Creek Mounds.

Hunting Deer, turkey, quail, and other game. State license required. During hunting season, primitive camping allowed only at designated sites and requires a permit in some parts of these forests.

Fishing Bream, bass, catfish, bluegill, and shellcracker in numerous lakes. State license required.

ADMINISTRATIVE OFFICES

Forest Headquarters 100 W. Capitol St., Suite 1141, Jackson, MS 39269 (601) 965-4391

Bienville Ranger District Route 2, Box 268A, Forest, MS 39074 (601) 469-3811

Strong River Ranger District 214 Mimosa St. (Hwy. 35N) P. O. Box 217, Raleigh, MS 39153 (601) 782-4271

Holly Springs Ranger District Hwy. 78 East, Box 400, Holly Springs, MS 38635 (601) 252-2633

Tombigbee Ranger District Route 1, Box 98 A, Ackerman, MS 39735 (601) 285-3264

Delta • Homochitto
NATIONAL FORESTS DIRECTORY

POINTS OF INTEREST

Blue Lake Recreation Area Primitive camping in the Delta Forest with a one-mile loop hiking trail. A good area to watch wildlife. Take State Route 16 south from Rolling Fork. Turn right on Forest Service Road 715.

Clear Springs Recreation Area A twelve-acre lake fed by springs on the Homochitto Forest. There are twenty-two campsites and two hiking trails. Go east from Natchez on U. S. Highway 84/98. Turn right or south on County Road 104 near Meadville. Travel about four miles to the recreation area entrance.

RECREATIONAL OPPORTUNITIES

Hiking and Riding Several scenic trails near key recreation areas.

Camping and Picnicking Eighty primitive campsites in the Delta Forest. Reservations are required during hunting season. Pipes Lake on the Homochitto is a nice spot for picnics.

Hunting Deer, turkey, quail, waterfowl, and other game. Hunting is extremely active in both forests. During the season, only duck hunters are allowed in Greentree Reservoirs.

Canoeing Black Creek in the DeSoto National Forest. PHOTO COURTESY OF USDA FOREST SERVICE

Fishing Bass, crappie, bream, catfish and others. State license required.

Off-Road Vehicles Many designated all-terrain vehicle roads on the Delta Forest. Ask for maps at ranger station.

ADMINISTRATIVE OFFICES

Forest Headquarters 100 W. Capitol St., Suite 1141, Jackson, MS 39269 (601) 965-4391

Delta Ranger District Sharkey-Ag. Bldg., 402 Hwy. 61 North, Rolling Fork, MS 39159 (601) 873-6256

Homochitto Ranger District 950 Hwy., 24 E. Box 398, Gloster, MS 39638 (601) 225-4281

Bude Ranger District Route 1, Box 1, Meadville, MS 39653 (601) 384-5876

Mount Magazine, in the Ozark National Forest, is the tallest peak between the Rockies and Appalachian Mountains. Surrounded by picturesque valleys, the panoramic view from the summit takes in two Arkansas mountain ranges—the Ouachita and Ozarks. Visitors can hike or drive to the top, where magnificent bluffs and sturdy red cedars are among the attractions. LAURENCE PARENT

Ozark
AND
St. Francis

N A T I O N A L F O R E S T S

From caves to crests

The Ozark National Forest in northwest Arkansas has striking features to explore both above and below ground. From the craggy bluffs of the state's highest point on Mount Magazine to the underworld sculptures in the depths of Blanchard Springs Caverns, the Ozark is fascinating in its diversity. Mountaineers, some descendants of rugged homesteaders, are part of the region's appeal, particularly their folk music. From April to November, the night air along many winding roads is filled with the sounds of fiddles and voices retracing timeless melodies.

For thousands of years, people have made their homes in the Ozark Mountains, actually part of the Boston Mountains, an eroded plateau uplifted millions of years ago. French explorer Du Tisne named the area when he described an Indian tribe he met as "aux aurcs," or "with bows." The Anglicized version became Ozarks. Spanish conquistador Hernando de Soto also found his way to these Arkansas mountains in the mid 1500s, but the first white settlement didn't take root until 1810. Word of superb hunting in the virgin oak and hickory forests soon spread, however. Indeed, Arkansas became known as the Bear State. So many hunters descended on the territory, however, that by the late 1800s there was concern that not a single black bear remained. Like the bear, the trees were also used with little thought of tomorrow. Woods were cut acre after acre, then soils repeatedly burned, preventing new trees from sprouting. Without the thick network of tree roots to hold soils in place, ridgetops eroded, silting streams and rivers, killing fish and other species dependent on clear water. This was the same predictable story repeated over and again across the nation, until conservationists sounded the alarm and government stepped into action. The Ozark National Forest, formed in 1908, was among the first established in the eastern United States.

Now watersheds are monitored and protected, with more than 1,000 miles of perennial streams originating in the forest, which also has sections of the Mulberry River, designated wild and scenic, and the Buffalo River, noted for recreation. The White River, where a record-breaking thirty-eight-pound brown trout was caught in 1988, also touches part of the forest. Hardwoods, predominantly oaks and hickories, cover about sixty percent of the Ozark's 1.2 million acres, with shortleaf pine comprising much of the rest. While their numbers are fewer, dogwoods and redbuds are sprinkled among the other trees, coloring the springtime woods in crisp white and deep rose blooms. Altogether, more than 500 woody plant species can be found. Wildlife is also diverse. There are nearly ninety species of birds considered common or fairly common in the Ozark National Forest, including the comical roadrunner, whose feet barely touch the ground as he races about. Songbirds are especially abundant, particularly indigo buntings, goldfinches, and cardinals. Bald eagles are also seen in the forest. And following the reintroduction of 263 black bears in Arkansas in 1963, the state-wide population has increased to about 2,000.

Among the more exotic creatures making their homes in the Ozark are three kinds of rare bats: the Indiana, Gray, and Ozark Big-eared, all classified as sensitive species. These mammals are drawn to the region because of the limestone bedrock of the Ozark Mountains, marked by sheltered rock overhangs and caves where the bats can retreat for daytime sleep and winter hibernation. Blanchard Springs Caverns north of Mountain View is easily the most spectacular of these habitats and one of the most accessible in the southern national forests.

Open for tours year-round, the caverns, estimated to be between fifty and seventy million years old, contain exceptional speleothems or formations. The stark beauty of giant flowstones, columns, draperies, and other mineral forms draws about 110,000 tourists annually. And while visitors are not guaranteed to see a bat in the caverns, stuffed specimens are displayed and explained in an educational exhibit in the visitor

Black bears were hunted almost out of existence in Arkansas, but are making a comeback. Wildlife biologists use radio collars and other methods to track them and study their habits. BILL LEA

center. Facts about these misunderstood creatures are entertainingly presented, including their benefit as mosquito eaters. Other cave dwellers, blind after generations spent in the dark, are also examined, such as the Ozark salamander and blind crayfish. The exhibit and a short movie, "The World Down Below," are worthwhile introductions before boarding the elevator to descend 216 feet into the caverns.

Unlike many well-known caves in the United States, Blanchard Springs Caverns are still alive, meaning speleothems continue to form. The process begins as groundwater containing carbonic acid percolates down through cracks in the calcite-enriched limestone layers. As it passes through the limestone, the water dissolves the calcite, and when this acid liquid meets cave air, carbon dioxide is released. The water then deposits the calcite, layer by layer, in slow drops within the cave. Thousands—perhaps millions—of years may pass while the calcite steadily builds into more stalactites, stalagmites, and other formations to further decorate the underworld rooms. Variables, especially the amount of rainfall, influence the rate of development, and while they can't be certain, geologists theorize that the oldest formation may be between two and five million years old. Blanchard Springs Caverns offers the rare chance to watch this geological phenomenon.

Dramatic lighting artfully illuminates the other-worldly features found along the Dripstone Trail. This trail, one of two, explores the upper level of the cave's two layers and is accessible to all ages and abilities, including those in wheelchairs. Forest Service guides lead visitors along a paved path

about a half-mile long, passing close by many formation types in two cave rooms, one of which is big enough to hold three football fields. The air is damp and cool, a constant fifty-eight degrees, and there are subtle but noticeable differences in the colors of the subterranean environment. Varying shades of white are found where calcite is the dominant mineral deposited in the speleothems. But when manganese is present, formations take on shades of blue, black, and gray. Brown, yellow, and red coloring indicate iron oxides are present.

The second tour, the Discovery Trail, courses for

Above: Roadrunners rarely fly, relying instead on fast feet to chase lizards, snakes, and insects. These birds are fairly common in the Ozark National Forest. BILL LEA
Right: The crimson berries of dogwoods provide important autumn food for cedar waxwings and other birds. ADAM JONES

more than a mile through the lower level and is not advised for anyone with respiratory or walking problems because of its nearly 700 steps. Fewer speleothems have formed in this younger part of Blanchard Springs Caverns, but one that has, the Giant Flowstone, is possibly the largest of its kind anywhere. Along this route, visitors will see the underground stream that eventually empties into Blanchard Springs at one of the cave's two natural entrances. And they will see the campsites of early explorers, twentieth-century adventurers who followed the first known visitor by more than a thousand years (see sidebar story). The Discovery Trail is offered only during summer months, in part to protect hibernating bats in the cave's lower reaches.

Camping is so popular at the adjoining Blanchard Springs Recreation Area that a three-night limit is necessary. Nearby Gunner Pool Recreation Area, however, has a two-week limit, like most other forest campgrounds. Swimming and fishing are possible at both spots, and each has a trailhead to the North Sylamore Creek Trail, which follows the meandering waters with wild and scenic designation for about fifteen miles.

Hiking trails twist and turn throughout the Ozark National Forest, many of them skirting rocky creeks that spill over waterfalls, forming deep basins ideal for an impromptu dip. The longest and best known is the Ozark Highlands Trail that stretches for 161 miles

Blanchard Springs flows from one of two natural entrances to Blanchard Springs Caverns in the Ozark National Forest. Inside the caverns, visitors see the underground stream that forms the springs.
EARL NOTTINGHAM

UNDERGROUND EXPLORERS

Deposited in countless layers by ancient seas, the shells of marine animals were gradually compacted and transformed into the limestone karst area of springs, sinkholes, and caves of Blanchard Springs Caverns in the Ozark National Forest. Discovery of this cave's wonders is a story unfolding over many years.

Early white settlers apparently avoided the place, put off, per-haps, by the breakneck drop in one sinkhole entrance or by the rushing spring at the other opening. Not until 1934 did a Forest Service employee, with help from Civilian Conservation Corpsmen, descend by ropes through the sinkhole. But even he didn't travel far into the cave, which remained largely unexamined for another twenty years. Finally, in 1955, five more adventurers lowered themselves into the darkness and began the first of their many journeys through the caverns.

Imagine their shock when they discovered signs that someone else had reached the deep recesses long before them. A skull, scattered bones, and charred reeds, probably burned for light, were all that remained of a Native American who had entered the cave about a thousand years before. Why he was there and how he died are just two of the many unanswered mysteries of Blanchard Springs Caverns.

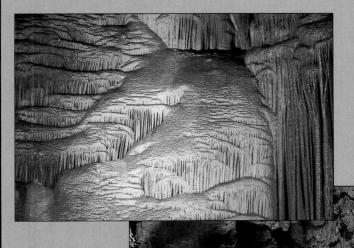

Left: Plan to see the flowstones on the Discovery Trail in summer because the lower caverns are closed in winter to protect bats. PHOTO COURTESY OF USDA FOREST SERVICE
Below: Towering three stories, the Giant Column in the Cathedral Room is one of many other-worldly sights along the Dripstone Trail. Special lighting accents the formations. PHOTO COURTESY OF USDA FOREST SERVICE

across northern Arkansas from near the Oklahoma border to the Buffalo National River. The trail passes many of the forest's recreation spots, including Big Piney Creek, one of the Ozark's largest free-flowing streams. Big Piney Creek is prized for its smallmouth and largemouth bass, sunfish, and catfish, and is also a favorite for canoeists in spring when waters are high enough for navigation (float trip planners for any of the Ozark's creeks or rivers should consider seasonal water fluctuations, which can be significant).

To the south and west of Blanchard Springs Caverns lies another geological point of interest, Alum Cove Natural Bridge. A quartz-sandstone cave eroded by wind, rain, and ice was transformed into this massive arch more than 130 feet long and twelve feet thick. A national recreation trail loops in an easy hike to the bridge and along a bluff where Native American hunters camped. Sassafras, black cherry, sweetgum, white ash, and American beech are just a few of the trees lining the walk. In spring, lacy white blossoms of the serviceberry tree mix with the dogwoods and redbuds, while in summer the understory is colored by fragrant yellow foxglove and showy white hydrangeas.

The bridge and a number of other recreation sites are near the Arkansas Highway Scenic 7

Above: Scaling Sam's Throne, a stool-shaped formation, challenges rock climbers in the Ozark National Forest. PHOTO COURTESY OF USDA FOREST SERVICE - TIM ERNST

Left: Alum Cove Natural Bridge is more than 130 feet long and twelve feet thick. An easy trail leads to the arch and continues past cave-like rooms. KEN GUSTON

Right: Richland Creek, one of six rivers designated as wild and scenic in the Ozark National Forest, flows through the Richland Creek Wilderness. Arkansas is renown for its cold, clear creeks and streams, which attract anglers from miles around. Canoeists also venture into the streams whenever water levels are favorable. PHOTO COURTESY OF USDA FOREST SERVICE - TIM ERNST

Byway, a north-south route that travels through the forest for about thirty-six miles. The "Scenic 7," which continues south through the Ouachita National Forest for another twenty-four miles, is an ideal pathway for an overview of the topography and vegetation of Arkansas, touted as "the Natural State." Rated one of the ten most scenic drives in America, the byway is part of a highway that starts at the Louisiana state line near El Dorado, Arkansas, and extends to the Missouri state line at Diamond City, Arkansas. Brochures about points of interest along the route are available from ranger offices in both forests. Funded by spouses of Rotary Club members, the Rotary Ann pull-off and picnic area in the Ozark National Forest is among the best vantage points, especially in fall when hardwood trees are in full color.

Just off the byway on State Highway 16 in the Ozark National Forest stands Pedestal Rocks, one of many special interest areas. Unusual rock formations rim a deep, narrow canyon dense with oaks and hickories. A wooded trail slopes gently for a mile to the rim where immense flat rocks jut out through the air like tabletops for giants. A darker, more mysterious environment exists just below the rocks, which create deep shelters. The overhangs provide dry refuge from sudden summer showers that can spring up unexpectedly, then pass just as quickly.

Water sports are the lure at Shores Lake, formed from a dam on Hurricane Creek built by the Civilian Conservation Corps in the 1930s. There is a shady campground near the eighty-two-acre lake. More of the CCC's handiwork, rustic stone and wood cabins, have been refurbished near Shores Lake on White Rock Mountain. A fifteen-mile loop trail, recently built by teenage volunteers, climbs from the lake to the top of the rugged mountain where hikers can rent one of three cabins or stay in a small campground. The cabins are a short walk from a clearing with a panoramic view of the forest. A lodge for groups is also available and its basement is expected to be open as a

hostel for hikers in 1993. Many couples have been married in the open air here and returned for years after on anniversaries. The mountain's caretakers are no longer surprised by the nuptials, or most other happenings on their isolated peak (see sidebar story).

Volunteers were also important in the recent restoration of ten rental cabins built in another federal government relief program funded by the Works Progress Administration at Lake Wedington. The 102-acre lake, in a northwestern corner of the forest near Fayetteville, is part of a recreation area for water sports, camping, and picnicking.

Cove Lake, near the base of Mount Magazine, also offers water sports, camping, and picnic areas. In summer, the Forest Service presents free interpretive nature programs in the Cove Lake Campground. Avid hikers enjoy the nearly eleven-mile trail from the lake to Cameron Bluff Campground atop the mountain. The highest mountain between the Alleghenies and Rocky Mountains at 2,753 feet, Mount Magazine is the only Ozark National Forest recreation center south of Interstate 40. With clear skies, the view encompasses the snaking Arkansas River to the north and the Ouachita Mountains to the south.

BEARS, BRIDES, AND BIRDS

Don't let Paula and Jack White fool you into believing that White Rock Mountain is named after them, even though they live there. It's the color of the rock bluffs that gives the peak its name. But other tales shared by this friendly couple are based in fact, like their delightful descriptions of a frequent caller, a black bear standing six feet tall and weighing 300 pounds or more. Paula White has proof to back up this tale—a photograph she took of the garbage-plundering bruin.

Some might find life lonely at 2,300 feet in the air and far from the nearest town, but not the Whites, who occupy a frame house once used by Forest Service employees as a mountaintop fire lookout. For company, they have an affectionate assortment of cats and dogs, and from spring to fall, hummingbirds hover three and four at a time around their porch feeder. Nor is there any shortage of human callers, many of whom have journeyed to the mountaintop for much of their lives. Honeymoon-

Visitors to White Rock Mountain can rent three log cabins and this beautiful 1930s vintage lodge. PHOTO COURTESY OF USDA FOREST SERVICE - TIM ERNST

ers often start their marriages on White Rock Mountain and return for years.

The Whites rent and maintain the cabins and lodge for the Forest Service, a job they decided to pursue after visiting the Ozark mountains themselves. Inevitably, guests find they forgot something, and to spare them the long drive to the nearest store, the Whites will good-naturedly loan

what they can. On occasion, this may include one of their pets, when visitors, lonesome for their own cats and dogs, find themselves attached to the Whites' willing critters for the duration of their stay. The hospitality has even extended to the loan of inanimate creatures when a little boy, distraught that he had left his teddy bear behind, was allowed to adopt Paula's stuffed teddy.

Oaks reflecting off the Mulberry River accentuate the spectacular colors of autumn in the Boston Mountains. THOMAS RITTER

St. Francis

To the east on the Arkansas border with Mississippi lies the St. Francis National Forest, established in 1960. Only about 21,000 acres, the St. Francis is managed with the Ozark. Together, the two produce more than forty-nine million board feet of timber annually. Renowned for two large recreation lakes, Bear Creek and Storm Creek, the St. Francis takes its name from the river flowing along its eastern edge. The Mississippi and L'Anguille rivers also span part of the forest. All this water makes the St. Francis an angler's haven for bass, crappie, catfish, and bream. Much of the forest lies on Crowley's Ridge, which starts in Illinois and continues through Missouri and into Ar-

kansas, a span of almost 200 miles. Within the St. Francis, the ridge rises about 100 feet above the delta lands and is two to three miles wide. Oaks and hickories, as well as poplars, American beeches, cypresses, swamp black gums, and sycamores are found in the St. Francis, which has one of the largest hardwood stands in Arkansas. Fertile bottomlands in the forest contain alluvial soils as deep as 200 feet.

The St. Francis Scenic Byway travels twenty miles through the forest, providing both fine views of the hardwoods and access to the two lakes. There are two campgrounds at 625-acre Bear Creek Lake near Marianna and a three-mile loop trail along the lakeshore.

Bear Creek is considered one of the state's finest fishing spots. Birdwatchers also enjoy the lake, which, like Storm Creek Lake farther south near Helena, is along the migratory Mississippi flyway. Canada geese and other waterfowl stop over in the forest's waters on their seasonal journeys north and south.

A rare feature near Storm Creek Lake, which also has a campground near the lakeshore, is a Research Natural Area where century-old trees somehow escaped early loggers. Huge specimens, with diameters as big as three feet, can be found within the area's 400 acres. The Forest Service prohibits any logging within the area so that researchers—and visitors—can observe a slice of nature unfolding without intervention. Similarly, little is done in the Ozark's five wilderness areas that might alter them, and anyone who enters is urged to leave no evidence of the journey so that others may sample a bit of untamed country. ♣

The sunny petals of daisies mix with crown vetch blossoms in a summer floral display. Crown vetch, introduced by Europeans, is often planted to prevent erosion. ADAM JONES

Ozark • St. Francis
NATIONAL FORESTS DIRECTORY

POINTS OF INTEREST

Geological Interest Areas Located throughout the forest and identified on forest maps. Alum Cove Natural Bridge, Buzzard Roost Rocks, Devil's Canyon, Pedestal Rocks, Sam's Throne, and Clifty Canyon are a few of many.

Blanchard Springs Caverns Guided tours, every day April 1 - October 30 and Wednesday through Sunday Nov. 1 - March 31, except federal holidays. Buy tickets and see an introductory film and exhibits in the visitor center, which also has informative books for sale. P. O. Box 1279, Mountain View, AR 72560 (501) 757-2211.

Ozark Folk Center and State Park Experts demonstrate old-time skills like basket making and blacksmithing. Folk musicians and dancers entertain nightly. Lodging, swimming pool, and restaurant are part of the park near Blanchard Springs Caverns. P. O. Box 500, Mountain View, AR 72560 (505) 269-3851.

WILDERNESS

Upper Buffalo 11,094 acres north of Clarksville, with the headwaters of the Buffalo River. Rugged, steep terrain, deep valleys, and forested hills.

Hurricane Creek 15,177 acres north of Russellville, almost over-used by visitors drawn to its sandstone bluffs and famed creek.

Richland Creek 11,822 acres northeast of Russellville, with a lovely creek and many towering vistas.

East Fork 10,777 acres in Pope County off Highway 27, characterized by hills and hollows and clear streams.

Leatherwood 16,956 acres northwest of Mountain View, an area of steep terrain bounded by the Buffalo National River.

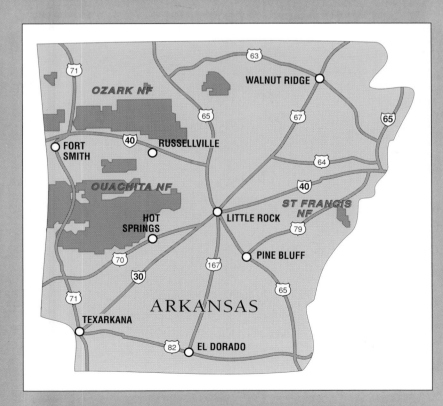

RECREATIONAL OPPORTUNITIES

Hiking and Riding More than 300 miles of trails. The 161-mile Ozark Highlands Trail is the longest of numerous developed hiking routes, from easy loops to strenuous mountain climbs. Horseback riders share the trail with hikers and mountain bikers on the new Moccasin Gap Horse Trail, twenty-eight miles long, with primitive campground. Horse trails also found on the Sylamore and Magazine Ranger Districts and at Devil's Den State Park.

Camping More than two dozen campgrounds with more than 300 sites in combined Ozark and St. Francis Forests, some open only seasonally. Dispersed camping permitted unless posted otherwise.

Cabins and Lodge White Rock Mountain open year-round. (501) 667-1248 Lake Wedington open year-round. (501) 442-9268.

Hunting White-tailed deer, turkey, squirrel, and other game. Licenses issued by Arkansas Game and Fish Commission.

Fishing More than 1,000 miles of streams and excellent river and lake fishing for bass, crappie, sunfish, catfish, and trout. Licenses issued by Arkansas Game and Fish Commission.

Off-Road Vehicles Only on open forest roads.

SCENIC DRIVES

Pig Trail Scenic Byway Named for meandering, pig-trail course and because it's a route to the University of Arkansas, home of the Razorbacks.

Mount Magazine Scenic Byway Crosses the top of Mount Magazine, highest point in Arkansas. Overlooks the Arkansas River Valley. Access to Cove Lake and Mount Magazine Recreation Area.

Ozark Highlands Scenic Byway Travels a ridge between headwaters of major streams and gives access to Ozone Recreation Area and Ozark Highlands Trail. Abundant wildlife includes deer, turkey, and bear.

Arkansas Scenic 7 Byway Sixty miles, passing through the Ozark and Ouachita National Forests. Access to Alum Cove Natural Bridge, Pedestal Rocks, Ozark Highlands Trail and many other recreation spots.

Sylamore Scenic Byway Blanchard Springs Caverns is the best-known attraction along a road maintained for visual appeal. Limestone bluffs, winding stream, and oak and hickory forest dominate the landscape.

St. Francis Scenic Byway Part state highway, part Forest Service road, byway passes over Crowley's Ridge for more than twenty-one miles.

ADMINISTRATIVE OFFICES

Headquarters (both forests) P.O. Box 1008, 605 W. Main Street, Russellville, AR 72801 (501) 968-2354

Bayou Ranger District Route 1, Box 36, Hector, AR 72843 (501) 284-3150

Boston Mountain Ranger District Highway 23 North, P.O. Box 76, Ozark, AR 72949 (501) 667-2191

Buffalo Ranger District P.O. Box 427, Highway 7 North, Jasper, AR 72641 (501) 446-5122

Magazine Ranger District Highway 22 East & Kalamazoo Road, P.O. Box 511, Paris, AR 72855 (501) 963-3076

Pleasant Hill Ranger District Highway 21 North, P.O. Box 190, Clarksville, AR 72830 (501)754-2864

Sylamore Ranger District Highway 14, North, Henderson Bldg., P.O. Box 1279, Mountain View AR 72560 (501) 269-3228

St. Francis Ranger District Route 4, Box 14-A, Marianna, AR 72360, (501) 295-5278

Cass Civilian Conservation Center Highway 23 North, HC 63. Box 219, Ozark, AR 72949 (501) 667-3686

Lake Ouachita, in the center of the Ouachita National Forest, is a magnet for recreation in Arkansas. Clean water and a wooded setting make the 48,300-acre lake popular for swimming, sailing, skiing, and fishing. The Ouachita River, favored by canoers, spills into the western corner of the lake, which is encircled by the rounded peaks of the Ouachita Mountains. MATT BRADLEY

Ouachita

Arkansas diamond

The Little Missouri River in western Arkansas flows clear and cool through the Ouachita National Forest. Visitors, drawn by the water, set up their tents and camp stoves nearby in Albert Pike Campground. Throughout a hot summer day, all ages wade from the smooth gravel beach out into the slow-moving river pools. Children haul and stack rocks to form a channel near the shallows, then float repeatedly in their inner tubes down its length, stopping only when the call comes for mealtime. Their rock structure will remain in place long after the youngsters have gone home, but not indefinitely. Heavy spring rains will turn the lazy Little Missouri of summer into a raging torrent and scatter the rocks like pebbles. A different set of visitors will venture into the river then, thrillseekers ready for a rollicking canoe ride as long as twenty miles.

With forty-five shady sites, Albert Pike Campground is the starting point for many forms of recreation in the Ouachita. An interpretive nature trail begins here, and informative programs are presented by Forest Service interpreters in an amphitheater in summer. Similar facilities are spread throughout the forest, which has more than thirty campgrounds, many near water and other recreational opportunities.

The South's oldest and largest national forest, the Ouachita is located mainly in west-central Arkansas, with portions of its 1.6 million acres extending into eastern Oklahoma. A mixture of pine and hardwood trees grows in the forest, which is a center for forestry research as well as an important source of timber, with about 150 million board feet harvested annually. The name "Ouachita" (pronounced WASH-it-tah) is attributed to early French explorers and their spelling of an Indian word meaning, "good hunting grounds." Mountains running through the forest are also called Ouachita. Unlike most North American ranges, the Ouachita Mountains are oriented to the east and west. Among the oldest mountains in the East and the highest range between the Appalachians and Rockies, the Ouachita peaks were pinched and faulted long ago by collisions of the earth's plates.

The Ouachita's southern portion, which includes Albert Pike Campground, contains a varied selection of recreational opportunities. The Little Missouri River Trail, for example, starts at Albert Pike Campground and winds along the river, providing a look at the narrow valley and low mountains typical of this part of the forest. Huge novaculite boulders along the path are interspersed with old-growth trees like eastern red cedars and umbrella magnolias that stretch out over the banks of this designated wild and scenic river.

Hikers must ford the river and adjoining creeks several times, not a hard task in low water when stepping stones ease the way. There are plans to erect foot bridges at these spots and to lengthen the trail, which currently ends near the moderate slopes of Little Missouri Falls. This is another location favored on hot days by bathers who enjoy dashing in and out of the water tumbling over the rocks.

Near the falls, a more challenging hike beckons on the Athens-Big Fork Trail, which climbs three mountains. Following part of an old postal route, the trail is a reminder of just how tough early mail carriers were. The Winding Stairs Trail, just southwest of Albert Pike, is another strenuous hike more than three miles long. No vehicles are permitted near this stretch of the river, resulting in fewer visitors. Bold rock outcrops, waterfalls, and deep pools ideal for fish are the hiker's reward, along with the chance to see bald and golden eagles. In winter, as many as sixty bald eagles have been counted in the area within the scope of only a few hours. Not far away, the Cossatot River, also distinguished with wild and scenic status, is similarly marked by rocky stretches and restive pools.

Driving is another way to enjoy the Ouachita, and often one of the best activities for seeing wildlife, particularly deer. From Albert Pike Campground, Forest Service Road 106 travels a picturesque route toward Bard Springs. Scarlet tanagers, red-eyed vireos, indigo buntings, and many other birds flit through the leaf

The Upper Kiamichi River Wilderness is visible from the Talimena Scenic Byway in the western part of the forest in Oklahoma.
LAURENCE PARENT

cover; depending on the season, purple cone flowers, yellow lady slippers, and other wildflowers bloom on the roadsides. Lovely American beech trees with smooth, mottled gray trunks also grow along the way.

The drive passes the Leader Mountain Walk-In Turkey Hunting Area, one of seven in the Ouachita. No vehicles are allowed for part of the year in these sections to preserve quiet for hunters and protect turkeys during nesting and raising of their young. The road also skirts Blaylock Creek, a small stream popular among dispersed campers, who may use such sites throughout the forest at no cost, with few restrictions. Stream-bank campers enjoy dropping their fishing lines into the water in hopes of catching something to cook and eat. Chances are, many will succeed. Fishing is excellent throughout the forest, particularly at Shady Lake, farther along on Forest Road 106. Bream, catfish, and bass are the favored sport fish in the twenty-five-acre lake. For those interested in learning more about the forest, there is a half-mile tree identification trail nearby. Several other trails are also in the vicinity, including hikes through the rugged Caney Creek Wilderness where elevations climb to 2,330 feet.

The Ouachita's most spectacular drive is farther west. The fifty-four-mile Talimena Scenic Byway follows high ridges with some of the best views in the state. Beginning near the town of Mena, the road travels Arkansas Highway 88, passing a Forest Service visitor information station offering guidebooks and other useful information about the area. A loop trail about three miles long at the center is popular with hikers and mountain bikers. From

Above: The dwarf blue flag iris prefers moist ground.
WILLIAM B. FOLSOM
Below: Shady Lake Recreation Area is a good spot for catching bream, catfish, and bass. PHOTO COURTESY OF USDA FOREST SERVICE

there, the scenic byway steadily climbs, eventually topping Rich Mountain, the second-highest peak in the state and, at 2,681 feet, the forest's highest point. Frequent pull-offs along the road provide panoramic views of the forest and distant mountains. A blue haze sometimes softens the scope in summer, but in fall, the air is crisp and the vistas clear and far. Trees, clothed in rich colors, fill the horizon. Wildflowers hug the roadsides, with the deep purple of tall ironweed and brilliant yellows of sunflowers predominating in summer. At this elevation, cooling breezes are common, even in August.

Black Fork Mountain Wilderness is one of the sights visible from the byway pull-offs. A six-mile trail travels through the wilderness, renowned for boulders as big as cars. So many of the boulders are spread successively across the ground that they are described as rock rivers.

At Rich Mountain's summit, the Talimena Scenic Byway enters Queen Wilhemina State Park, where there is a lodge, restaurant, campground, small-scale train, and miniature golf. The one-third-mile walk from the hotel to the Lover's Leap observation deck is fairly easy and offers another substantial view of the mountains and forest. There is also a short trail to a pioneer cemetery just beyond the state park. Deer, bear, and many birds live in the area, which is also

inhabited by bat colonies. At dusk, the darkening skies fill with legions of these creatures, chasing insects.

Beyond the state park, the byway re-enters the Ouachita National Forest and soon passes into Oklahoma where the road becomes Highway One. Stunted white oaks, some perhaps 200 years old, grow along the slow mountain descent. Near the bottom of the mountain stands the Robert S. Kerr Arboretum and Nature Center. This preserve of 8,000 acres exists for the study and protection of numerous plant species. There is an exhibit shelter with brief introductory signs and photographs pointing out what can be learned on three easy loop trails. Interpretive signs along the paths further explain different aspects of the environment, from the growth habits and characteristics of various trees to the importance of soils.

Altogether, the Ouachita has 2,500 native plant species, and the Forest Service has set aside various locations to protect those with special sensitivity, such as the Arkansas cabbage and cossatot leafcup. Old-growth pine and hardwoods on Blowout Mountain in Arkansas and ancient beech trees in the Beech Creek Scenic Area of Oklahoma are two other examples of protected sites.

Beyond the arboretum and not far from the scenic byway, there are more than 100 miles of horse trails in the Oklahoma portion of the forest. Equestrians can

Mountain biking is gaining enthusiasts in the Ouachita National Forest where the Ouachita range has relatively gentle slopes.
PHOTO COURTESY OF USDA
FOREST SERVICE

Ecosystem management, now the order of business throughout the national forests, was officially inaugurated in a few sections of the country several years ago. The Ouachita was one of the proving grounds in the Southern Region for this new approach to tending the vital public resources of the national forests.

As a "New Perspectives" forest, the Ouachita has been experimenting with techniques taking into account the entire ecosystem—vegetation, wildlife, soils, water, air—all the components of the environment. Understanding and nurturing the relationships and processes binding these elements and the roles they play in maintaining the health of one another are the subjects of intense focus.

While caretakers of the nation's forests have practiced some ecosystem management steps under other names for many years, there are significant changes. An important new direction, for example, is the reduction, and in some instances elimination, of clearcutting. Previously, loggers regularly felled trees over fifteen to forty acres at a time, the cheapest and fastest method of harvesting. The results were unsightly voids. Mounting public outcry helped influence the move from clearcutting to other harvesting methods. For example, loggers may now be directed to thin selected trees from a stand, instead of taking them all.

Other efforts involve protecting the few remaining old-growth stands and promoting policies that will enable some of today's trees to become the old-growth forests of the future. The use of herbicides has also been reduced.

Ongoing research is likely to foster other changes. About thirty-five scientists are studying the Ouachita and forest managers are actively seeking increased public involvement in developing management strategies compatible with timber harvesting, hunting, and other uses provided on the forest.

---

choose from seven different trails of varying difficulty, and also make use of a campground designated for them and their horses. Other horse trails, some shared with mountain bikers, are located on the Arkansas side of the forest.

Near the end of the Talimena Scenic Byway, there is a visitor information station, a high bluff popular with hang gliders, and the Talihina State Park.

Running north and south in the eastern part of the forest is Arkansas Highway Seven Scenic Byway, also noted for wildflowers. The highway passes near Flatside Wilderness and Iron Springs Campground where there is access to good hiking trails.

Another worthwhile drive is Forest Service Road W20, not far from U.S. Highway 270 near the center of the forest. The road climbs Hickory Nut Mountain to an observation point high above Lake Ouachita. From the mountaintop, the 48,300-acre lake glimmering in the sunlight appears deceptively calm—for closer to the shore, the waters may churn with activity. Swimming, sailing, skiing, boating, and fishing draw thousands every year, creating one of the state's biggest vacation arenas. Lake Ouachita, considered among the cleanest lakes in the country, is managed by the U.S. Army Corps of Engineers, which also operates lakeside campgrounds. Much of the surrounding landscape, however, falls within the Ouachita National Forest.

The Ouachita River spills into the western side of the lake and is a favorite among canoeists, who can float forty-five miles down the river from Pine Ridge on national forest land. Both calm and swirling waters mark the course and there are four float camps with restrooms, water, and campsites along the way. High spring waters can create dangerous conditions for the unwary, but the river is fairly tame in summer and fall. Rocky bluffs and overhanging trees create pockets of deep green shade, welcome in Arkansas' often blistering summers. But even when the sunshine sizzles, the river, for those who fall in, is icy cold. Anglers are attracted by the water's white bass, which make their spring spawning runs along its path.

The Ouachita is also a magnet for rock and mineral hunters, from professional miners to amateurs interested in finding specimens for themselves. The forest's bounty of quartz crystals was first discovered by Indians, who used the glass-like minerals for tools and

come to collect crystals in the forest without charge, but should check with the ranger office before beginning their search so they won't interfere with any of the fifty commercial mines leased in the forest.

Among the historical points of interest in the forest is a former Girl Scout camp with native stone and wood cabins and a great hall listed on the National Register of Historic Places. The camp is only a short walk from another of the Ouachita's clear lakes, Lake Sylvia. There is a campground on the shore of this sixteen-acre lake and two interpretive trails, one accessible to the physically disabled.

Some of the best long-distance hiking can be found on the Ouachita National Recreation Trail, which passes east to west across the forest for 192 miles. The trail's many access points also make it popular for shorter excursions. To reach the trail from Lake Sylvia requires hiking about half a mile. Another option involves a short drive along forest roads to the trailhead at Flatside Pinnacle. From there, go one way and the trail plunges into the Flatside Wilderness. Hike the other direction and the path leads steadily upwards along a rock-strewn corridor where a deer may leap into the brush or a flash of burnt orange may streak into the sky as a red-tailed hawk soars out of sight. A blue racer snake may be sunning itself on one of the wooden steps, quickly retreating into a knothole at the approach of footsteps. After less than a mile, the trail reaches Flatside Pinnacle at 1,550 feet. The rocky edge offers an unimpeded view for miles. Trees, mountains, water, and sky span the distance, the best of the Ouachita in a memorable composite. ♣

divining the future. Even today, some people think these "Arkansas diamonds" contain metaphysical powers, an impression that has helped fuel the value of the crystals and intensify market demand. A mineral band several miles wide stretches from Jessieville, Arkansas, into Oklahoma, and holds some of the richest quartz deposits in North America. Amateurs are wel-

Ouachita
NATIONAL FOREST DIRECTORY

POINTS OF INTEREST

Flatside Pinnacle A high bluff just outside the Flatside Wilderness on the Ouachita National Recreation Trail. Trailhead is less than a mile away on Forest Service Road 94.

Albert Pike Recreation Area Many recreation opportunities, including camping, swimming, fishing, and hiking. Winding Stairs Trail is nearby.

Take Arkansas State Highway 27 south from Mount Ida. Go west on State Highway 8. Follow Forest Road 43 past Little Missouri Falls to Forest Service Road 73. Head right and into the campground.

Robert S. Kerr Arboretum Located near the eastern Oklahoma border on Talimena Scenic Byway. Close by is the Winding Stair Mountain National Recreation Area with camping, horseback riding, a ninety-acre lake, and forty-five miles of the Ouachita National Recreation Trail.

WILDERNESS AREAS

Poteau Mountain, Arkansas 11,299 acres with high ridges reaching 2,406 feet. Located in the northern portion of the Ouachita, this wilderness is divided into two parts. In between is land managed similar to a wilderness but accessible by automobile.

Black Fork Mountain, Arkansas 8,430 acres, known for "rock rivers" and steep slopes.

Black Fork Mountain, Oklahoma 5,149 acres of rugged terrain and diverse plant species.

Caney Creek Wilderness, Arkansas 14,460 acres featuring a trail that follows Caney Creek across the wilderness. The 9.5-mile trail eventually crosses the wild and scenic Cossatot River. A connecting trail climbs Buckeye Mountain. Waterfalls and interesting rock formations.

Upper Kiamichi River, Oklahoma 10,819 acres with thickly forested ridges and varied vegetation. Ouachita National Scenic Trail passes through the wilderness, which is in the western portion of the forest.

Flatside, Arkansas 9,507 acres near the far eastern edge of the Ouachita. The most popular access point is on the Ouachita National Scenic Trail near Flatside Pinnacle. The trail leads to Crystal Prong, a creek, and a spring and then across the wilderness. For more solitude, enter from Forest Service Road 132.

Dry Creek, Arkansas 6,310 acres featuring numerous ridges and high sandstone bluffs. In the northern portion of the forest, the wilderness contains Chimney Rock, a large column that has broken away from a vertical rock wall.

RECREATIONAL OPPORTUNITIES

Hiking and riding Major campgrounds have interpretive trails. Numerous other hiking opportunities, including the 192-mile Ouachita National Recreation Trail. Miles of equestrian trails across the forest.

Camping More than thirty developed campgrounds. Most open from April through September. Selected areas remain open year round.

Scenic Drives Talimena Scenic Byway climbs high peaks in the western portion of the forest. Arkansas Highway 7, "Scenic Seven," winds north and south in the eastern part and continues north through the Ozark National Forest.

Rafting and canoeing Cossatot, Little Missouri, Caddo, and Ouachita Rivers are favored for float trips. Outfitters available to rent equipment.

Off-road vehicles Wolf Pen Gap Trails Complex is nine miles from Mena, Arkansas, on Highway 375. Mountain bikers ride these and other trails.

Shooting Free target ranges are located throughout the forest.

Hunting Game species include deer, turkey, squirrel, rabbit, racoon, quail, and various waterfowl. Arkansas Game and Fish Commission issues licenses.

Fishing Abundant smallmouth bass and longear sunfish in streams and channel catfish and bluegill in lakes and ponds.

ADMINISTRATIVE OFFICES

Forest Headquarters Federal Building, 100 Reserve Street, P.O. Box 1270, Hot Springs, AR 71902 (501) 321-5202

Caddo Ranger District P.O. Box 369, Glenwood, AR 71943 (501) 356-4186

Mena Ranger District Rt. 3, Box 220, Hwy. 71N, Mena, AR 71953 (501) 394-2382

Choctaw Ranger District HC 64, Box 3467, Heavener, OK 74937 (918) 653-2991

Oden Ranger District Route 9, Box 16, Oden, AR 71961 (501) 326-4322

Cold Springs Ranger District P.O. Box 417, Hwy. 10 E, Booneville, AR 72927 (501) 675-3233

Poteau Ranger District P.O. Box 2255, Waldron, AR 72958 (501) 637-4174

Fourche Ranger District Box 459, Hwy 10 E., Danville, AR 72833 (501) 495-2844

Tiak Ranger District P.O. Box 389, Idabel, OK 74745 (405) 286-6564

Jessieville Ranger District P.O. Box 189, Jessieville, AR 71949 (501) 984-5313

Winona Ranger District 1039 Hwy 10 N., Perryville, AR 72126 (501) 889-5176

Kiamichi Ranger District P.O. Box 577, Talihina, OK 74571 (918) 567-2326

Womble Ranger District P.O. Box 255, Mount Ida, AR 71957 (501) 867-2101

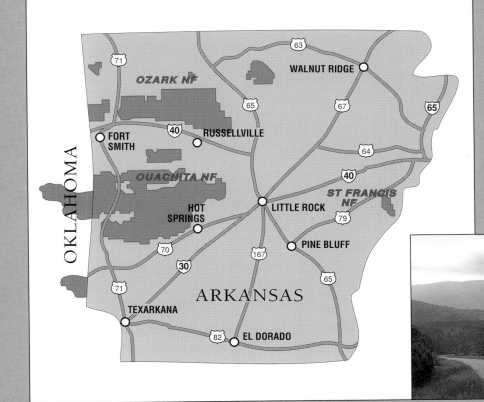

The Talimena Scenic Byway.
LAURENCE PARENT

Cypress trees are a common sight along Saline Bayou National Scenic River, part of the Kisatchie National Forest. The Kisatchie, however, includes much more than wet low lands. There is even a "Little Grand Canyon" with mesas, steep slopes, and sandstone outcrops more typically associated with the American West.
ROBERT W. PARVIN

Kisatchie

Bayous and blossoms

Caroline Dormon, a botanist and teacher, was a small woman with a big idea—establishing a national forest in Louisiana. Despite heated opposition, she persisted for years in lobbying politicians and trying to build public support. She even wrote the required legislation and proposed the forest's name. Now, Dormon is memorialized with a trail exploring the realization of her dream: the Kisatchie National Forest. The Caroline Dormon Hiking and Equestrian Trail ventures for thirteen miles through woodlands and along a bayou cherished by the crusader, who was also the first woman elected to the Society of American Foresters.

The Kisatchie, thought to be a Caddo Indian word for "cane country," is Louisiana's only national forest. Established in 1930, the Kisatchie includes over 600,000 acres managed in six ranger districts. Most of the acreage is in five large blocks in central Louisiana, with three smaller sections located in the northern part of the state. The canes that once bordered stream banks are long gone, swept away by floods in the early 1900s. Pines dominate, but hardwoods also thrive in the Coastal Plain soils and climate. In fact, growing conditions are so favorable that the Kisatchie is one of the most productive timberlands in the nation. There are also nineteen oil and gas wells in the forest and some gravel mining and cattle grazing.

The same conditions that promote tree growth are hospitable to other vegetation and wildlife, and the Kisatchie supports many different plants and animals. Along the Caroline Dormon Trail in central Louisiana, rabbits, coyotes, raccoons, roadrunners, and white-tailed deer may weave quickly in and out of view. Wildflowers are also plentiful, particularly the bright yellow petals of sunflowers and coreopsis. Hikers and riders can begin enjoying these and other sights along the trail from two starting points. One is beside the Longleaf Trail Scenic Byway. This seventeen-mile route is a worthwhile drive for seeing and learning about the forest.

Beginning near Natchitoches in the state's center, the byway heads west along the edge of the "Little Grand Canyon." The terrain here belies the widely held perception that all of Louisiana is flat swamps. There are steep slopes, mesas, and many sandstone cliffs and rock outcrops more typically associated with the West. The ancient sandstone's resistance to erosion has created the unexpected topography where petrified wood and fossils are found. Although eleva-

tions never climb much higher than 400 feet, there is a sense of much greater height, particularly from an overlook called Longleaf Vista. The Longleaf Vista Nature Trail is a 1.5-mile loop leading from the byway to the site, which is popular for picnics and equipped with restrooms and water. The easy walk highlights details about the area and passes the ruins of a nineteenth-century turpentine still. Other overlooks are spaced every few miles along the road.

The Longleaf Vista juts out into the rugged Kisatchie Hills Wilderness, also a favored place among hikers and horseback riders, who often enter along the Backbone Trail. The trail, over seven miles long, follows a ridge into the hills of the wilderness and has many excellent vantage points. Access to the Backbone Trail is also found along the scenic byway.

In addition to enjoying the scenery, drivers can discover the forest's natural attributes and history from a brochure available at the Kisatchie Ranger District office. Indians, Spaniards, the French, and English all left their imprint upon the land. Several places used by prehistoric peoples have been discovered within a mile of the byway, and for about two miles, the route follows part of the historic Military Road. Used some 200 years ago, this passageway led to Fort Jesup, at that time the "Gateway to the Western Frontier." Later, during the closing days of the Civil War, a tattered Southern Army retreated down the route and then used it to launch one final victorious assault.

Continuing west, the byway crosses Kisatchie Bayou, a state-designated scenic river. Kisatchie Bayou is sparkling-clear, with gurgling rapids and small waterfalls. Strewn with rocks and white sandbars, the bayou is an excellent place for wading or hopping across the water on stepping stones. Campers enjoy the Kisatchie Bayou Recreation Area on a bluff above the

Longleaf pines are valued commercially for their rapid growth and straightness, but they are also important habitat for endangered red-cockaded woodpeckers. The birds hollow out nests in live trees. C. C. LOCKWOOD

water. A second trailhead for the Caroline Dormon Trail is also found here.

Another sight along the byway is the Statesman Tree. About 175 years old, the pine is an example of lone trees that loggers sometimes left uncut in the early 1900s even as they were downing most trees for miles around. Under most circumstances, however, what they left untouched were the smaller or deformed trees, and two examples of these also remain just north of the byway between Forest Roads 311 and 135.

Northeast of the Kisatchie Bayou in another section of the forest is the Saline Bayou National Scenic River. Canoeists can float for nineteen miles down the bayou, easily observing many species of birds, and mammals such as gray or fox squirrels. Occasionally, alligators and snakes will be seen here lending to the traditional Louisiana "swamp mystique." During high water, however, the bayou can pour over its banks, making the journey hazardous. In late summer, low water can also impede travel. A check with the Winn Ranger District about water conditions is always advisable.

More often the trip is an easy ride, with glassy waters mirroring surrounding cypress trees. River banks are low, and with little underbrush in some stretches, views into the woods are far-reaching. Early morning and late afternoon offer the best chances for spotting wildlife, when small families of racoons may be marching single-file across logs. Mink, deer, and other animals also visit the water edges, as well as many birds. Look for the pileated woodpecker with its Woody Woodpecker topknot, echoing its constant pounding tattoo through the forest. Other crea-

Above: Tiny grass pink orchids, glistening with dew, have brief, but brilliant blooms in sunny locations. C.C. LOCKWOOD
Below: Kisatchie Bayou is sparkling clear, with small waterfalls and wide sandbars, perfect for sunbathing after a wade in the water. C. C. LOCKWOOD

PROTECTING THE SMALL AND LARGE

From a tiny water creature to a husky bear, imperiled residents of the Kisatchie National Forest are the focus of concerted protective efforts from forest managers. Wildlife biologists, for example, are surveying the forest's many streams to find the endangered Louisiana pearlshell mussel. Recently, they have located nine additional streams where the mussel exists, and these habitats will receive special attention. The Louisiana black bear is also dwindling in numbers to the extent that the bear has been under consideration for listing as a threatened species. Forest Service representatives are part of a tri-state committee seeking ways to protect and *enhance the bear population.*

Encouraging news is mounting in the forest for the endangered red-cockaded woodpecker. The number of bird colonies has remained fairly steady for several years, to the point that biologists have sent female birds to the national forests of Mississippi to boost declining colonies there. Kisatchie managers are also working to develop cooperative efforts between government and private industry to increase populations of the endangered woodpecker in Louisiana.

Forest Service employees examine endangered Louisiana pearlshell mussels.
C. C. LOCKWOOD

tures merit a note of caution: water moccasins and wasp nests sometimes lurk in overhanging branches.

The river passes through several distinct vegetative environments. In one stretch dominated by bluffs, moss-draped magnolias and catalpa trees grow, while in another darker region, cypress, oaks, and tupelo gums line the banks. The river corridor also supports many sensitive plants, including nine species rare to Louisiana that grow in the seventy-acre Saline Bayou Sandy Woodland Area. Overall, the Kisatchie hosts forty-six sensitive plants, including the yellow fringeless orchid, which opens its cluster of lemon yellow and orange blossoms in late summer.

Cloud Crossing Recreation Area is a favorite launching spot for float

Prescribed burning helps red-cockaded woodpeckers, which nest in trees banded in white. PHOTO COURTESY OF USDA FOREST SERVICE - JAMES R. CALDWELL

trips and a popular camping area. Other launch sites are under construction along the bayou, which eventually widens and slows to a crawl as it enters Saline Lake. These lower reaches of the bayou and the lake itself are often visited by egrets, blue herons, and wood ducks. Fishing is excellent in the waters, particularly for catfish, which can weigh more than thirty pounds. Alligator snapping turtles, some weighing 150 pounds, also may grab fishing lines with ferocious strikes.

Another designated scenic automobile route is located west of the Saline Bayou and north of Alexandria. The road winds through pine woods that look as if they have been dusted with snow when white dogwoods bloom for about a month, beginning in mid-March. The ten-mile Dogwood Auto Tour travels along Forest Road 120 and has several interpretive signs about the Kisatchie. Nearby is the National Catahoula Wildlife Management Preserve, part of which is restricted to foot travel. Deer and turkey hunters travel for miles to visit the preserve, one of the forest's best hunting grounds. Other visitors enjoy Stuart Lake Recreation Area nearby. Swimming and fishing are popular in the lake and there is an amphitheater for summer campground programs and a short nature trail.

Another campground is found at the most-visited recreation site in the forest, Kincaid Lake. This 2,600-acre lake, just southwest of Alexandria, has a beach that draws hundreds of sunbathers in the long, hot summers. Others enjoy skiing, swimming, and fishing. Hikers can spend days exploring a web of trails covering more than fifty miles, including the Wild Azalea National Recreation Trail. The trail crosses thirty-two miles adorned by hundreds of flowering shrubs and dogwoods.

Altogether, hikers on the Wild Azalea Trail can see six distinct plant communities, from prairies to bogs, to majestic stands of large bottomland hardwoods. The latter

are found in the Castor Creek Scenic Area where gigantic beeches and other aged specimens evoke the feeling of being in an outdoor cathedral. The Forest Service is developing sites along the way ideal for watching wildlife.

The Wild Azalea Trail has several significant off-shoots, including the Lakeshore Trail that wanders ten miles along Kincaid Lake, and another spur that leads

Above: Nesting boxes are often placed in national forests to attract wood ducks.
JOE MAC HUDSPETH

Below: Kincaid Lake Recreation Area is in central Louisiana, just southwest of Alexandria. PHOTO COURTESY OF USDA FOREST SERVICE - JAMES R. CALDWELL

to a campground. Oaks, hickories, and beeches grow along the way. Finally, the Wild Azalea Trail ends at Valentine Lake Recreation Area on the shores of another forty-six-acre lake.

The southernmost section of the Kisatchie lies south of Fort Polk Military Reservation. The principal attraction in this part of the forest is Fullerton Lake Recreation Area, built on the grounds of an old sawmill and mill town. In the early 1900s, Fullerton Mill was the largest pine sawmill west of the Mississippi River. Employees and their families numbered 5,000 and lived in the planned community. While only scattered ruins are still visible along the lakeshore, the Forest Service is developing exhibits to describe the abandoned mill and town. Once there were well laid-out streets and even a first-class hotel, and stores and offices were all under one roof in a precursor of the modern shopping mall.

There are several hiking trails of various lengths in the area. The longest is the ten-mile Whiskey Chitto Trail, named for a creek the path follows. The Whiskey Chitto connects with the Big Branch Trail, a loop open to both hikers and horseback riders. The Big Branch Trail moves through stands of old-growth pines in the Longleaf Scenic Area where endangered red-cockaded woodpeckers are found. The birds prefer to nest in cavities in living longleaf pines and are most visible near their nesting holes around sunrise and sunset.

Bogs are another feature of this section of the Kisatchie. Trees don't fare well in the moist soils and are often stunted. Usually dominated by grasses and sedges, bogs are also home to many flowering plants, including pitcher plants and sundews. These fascinating plants attract insects with bright blossoms, then capture and slowly digest them. Other plant species, many of them sensitive or rare, also grow in the bogs.

Lakes are the centers of recreation in the smaller sections of the Kisatchie farthest north. Corney Lake is the largest at 2,300 acres, and is trimmed with graceful bald cypress and water tupelos along the shore. Ducks and other wildlife are abundant in the area, as well as fish, drawing birdwatchers and other wildlife enthusiasts, also hunters and anglers. The other focus for recreation is at Caney Lakes, two bodies of water side by side. The 250-acre lower lake is a favorite with water skiers, who use a beach near a boat ramp to don their skis and glide into their rides across the water. The 125-acre upper lake, however, is off-limits to water skiers and power boats. Connected to the lower lake by a wide spillway, the upper waters are exceptionally calm. The stillness is only occasionally ruffled by the faint ripple of a canoe or the snap of an angler's fishing line.

Hikers, too, enjoy padding around in the quiet. The Sugar Cane National Recreation Trail loops around the lake for about seven miles and crosses a foot bridge over the spillway. Along the way, there is evidence of an old sugar mill, as well as the earthen terraces once built to stop erosion of old sugar cane fields. Wildflowers and beavers are among the other sights. ♣

The Wild Azalea National Recreation Trail explores many habitats. C.C. LOCKWOOD

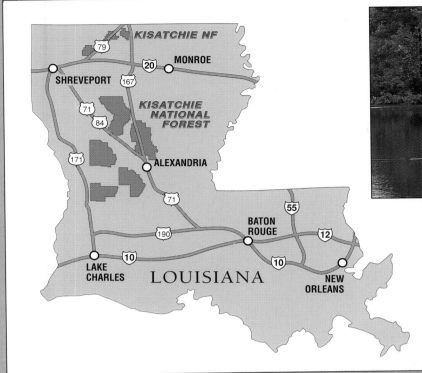

Upper reaches of Caney Lake are popular for quiet fishing. C. C. LOCKWOOD

Kisatchie
NATIONAL FOREST DIRECTORY

POINTS OF INTEREST

Longleaf Vista An overlook above Louisiana's "Little Grand Canyon" at the end of a mile-and-a-half interpretive trail. Take Interstate 49 northwest from Alexandria to Derry. Go south on State Hwy. 119. Turn right on Forest Road 59, the Longleaf Trail Scenic Byway.

Cloud Crossing A picnic area, primitive campground, and launching site for canoe trips on Saline Bayou. From Alexandria, take U. S. Hwy. 167 north to Dodson. Go west on State Hwy. 126. Turn left on State Hwy. 1233. Go west on Forest Road 513.

Kincaid Recreation Area A modern campground adjacent to a 2,600-acre lake. From Alexandria, drive west twelve miles on State Hwy. 28 to State Hwy. 121. Turn left and go one-fourth mile to Forest Road 279. Turn left and go three-and-one-half miles. Then turn left again on Forest Road 205.

WILDERNESS AREAS

Kisatchie Hills 8,700 acres of flat-topped mesas and sandstone cliffs in an area known as the "Little Grand Canyon."

RECREATION OPPORTUNITIES

Camping Numerous campgrounds equipped for both recreational vehicles and tent campers. In wildlife management areas, camping must be in designated areas during hunting seasons.

Hiking and Riding 140 miles of trails, including the Wild Azalea and Sugar Cane National Recreation Trails. There is horseback riding on the Caroline Dormon and Big Branch trails, in the wilderness, and along forest roads and old logging trails.

Scenic Drives The Longleaf Trail Scenic Byway is seventeen miles and has excellent vistas into the Kisatchie Hills Wilderness. A self-guided tour brochure explains some local history and attractions.

Canoeing Caney and Corney lakes and the Saline Bayou National Scenic River offer visually exciting float trips during most of the year.

Hunting Deer, squirrel, turkey, coyotes, quail, rabbit, waterfowl, woodcock, and other game. State licenses and regulations apply in most areas. An additional permit is required to hunt or fish in wildlife management preserves.

Fishing Largemouth bass, bluegill, sunfish, catfish, and others. State licenses and regulations apply. An additional permit is required in wildlife management preserves.

Off-Road Vehicles Allowed in much of the forest except where signs indicate the areas are off limits.

ADMINISTRATIVE OFFICES

Forest Headquarters 2500 Shreveport Hwy., Pineville, LA 71360 (318) 473-7160

Caney Ranger District P.O. Box 479, 324 Beardsley Street, Homer, LA 71040 (318) 927-2061

Catahoula Ranger District Route 1, Box 73, Bentley, LA 71407 (318) 765-3554

Evangeline Ranger District 3727 Government Street, Alexandria, LA 71302 (318) 445-9396

Kisatchie Ranger District P.O. Box 2128, Hwy. 6 West, Natchitoches, LA 71457 (318) 352-2568

Vernon Ranger District 3362 Lake Charles Hwy., Leesville, LA 71446 (318) 239-6576

Winn Ranger District P.O. Box 36, U. S. Hwy. 84 West, Route 3, Winnfield, LA 71483 (318) 628-4664

The wide-open spaces that made Texas famous can still be found in the four national forests and two grasslands. Profusions of garden coreopsis brighten summer meadows with their yellow and reddish-purple blooms, while pine woodlands provide shade from a blistering sun. ROBERT W. PARVIN

144

Texas

Lyndon B. Johnson • Caddo
Sabine • Angelina • Davy Crockett • Sam Houston

N A T I O N A L   G R A S S L A N D S   A N D   F O R E S T S

Cowboy country

Visions of the Old West come to life in the Caddo and Lyndon B. Johnson national grasslands in Texas. Forest Service managers in cowboy hats and chaps survey this territory on horseback, weaving around herds of grazing cattle. Texas straddles the unofficial dividing line between the southern and western United States, a position reflected in its national forests and grasslands. While the two grasslands are found in the typically western region of relatively flat and treeless land north of Dallas, the four forests in the "pineywoods" north of Houston are more representative of the East. Together, they comprise more than 670,000 acres.

Apart from feeding more than 1,500 cattle and supplying more than sixty-one million board feet of timber annually, the grasslands and forests are dotted with wells plumbing the rich reserves of oil and gas. There are oil and gas leases for more than 195,000 acres, mostly in the forests. Not all of the 140 wells produce income for the national forests, however, because some previous landowners retain mineral rights. Gravel is also mined. This tapping of natural resources coexists with extensive recreation by thousands of visitors every year.

Lyndon B. Johnson · Caddo

Wide-open spaces are what drew many into the land of the Lone Star state. They wanted distance between themselves and their neighbors, "elbow room" some called it. Many found what they sought on ground now part of the Lyndon B. Johnson and Caddo national grasslands. This is big sky country where the horizon extends for mile after mile. Windmills catch passing breezes and jackrabbits spring away with lightning speed. Bobcats, foxes, and coyotes also make their homes here.

In the 1800s, the grasslands were productive ranches and farms, but the soils gradually eroded into a nearly barren wasteland, part of the Dust Bowl that enveloped the region. Since the federal government began buying the land in the 1930s, efforts to revitalize the area have been underway. Fertilizing, planting grass, and building fences continues today, and the grasslands now provide important grazing land for privately owned livestock.

At only a little above 1,000 feet, Bald Knob Hill in the Lyndon B. Johnson National Grasslands may be one of the highest points in all of north central Texas. The LBJ covers 20,324 acres north of Fort Worth.

The 17,796-acre Caddo is divided into three parts, all in Fannin County. Sections overlook the Red River Valley and Oklahoma. While not abundant, there are trees in parts of the grasslands, including live oak, ashe juniper, red cedar, and Texas oak. Indians and pioneers used the junctures of trees and prairies as landmarks in the uncharted territory.

There are three lakes in the Caddo and two in the LBJ, all popular fishing spots for bream, catfish, and bass. Picnicking along the lakeshores is also common, as well as primitive camping. One of the lakes in the Caddo is named for Davy Crockett, the legendary frontiersman. Crockett supposedly camped nearby in what is now the town of Honey Grove. He and his band of Tennesseans enjoyed the local honey for several days, then continued on a journey that ultimately led to the battle of the Alamo and into Texas history.

Left: The Caddo and Lyndon B. Johnson national grasslands provide grazing land for privately-owned cattle. ROBERT W. PARVIN
Right: Fishing is excellent in the Angelina National Forest in East Texas. LAURENCE PARENT

Sabine · Angelina

Even at midday, little sunshine filters through the thick canopy of leaves from old trees soaring some 100 feet high in Mill Creek Cove. The immense trees, some four feet in diameter, are primarily mottled gray beeches and magnolias. Experts think this could be the only beech-magnolia climax forest in the entire western Gulf Coastal Plain, an area extending to Mobile, Alabama.

The cove is part of the 188,220-acre Sabine National Forest, which wraps around the Texas side of the Toledo Bend Reservoir. Formed by damming of the Sabine River, the reservoir is the fifth-largest built in the country and marks the Texas border with Louisiana.

The Sabine Forest, on its southwestern edge, also touches the Sam Rayburn Reservoir. The two lakes cover more than 296,000 acres and provide many of the forest's recreational opportunities. Sailboating, water skiing, and fishing are common, with bass weighing thirty pounds caught in Toledo Bend. Migrating waterfowl flock to the Sam Rayburn and Toledo Bend Reservoirs on their way south, and eagles spend the winter by the water. Velvety green wood ducks are year-round residents.

Overnight visitors to Toledo Bend have more than fifty lodging choices, from camping to hotels. The Forest Service maintains several campgrounds, including Ragtown Recreation Area on a high bluff overlooking the water. Red Hills Lake Recreation

Area is several miles away from the reservoir and has its own nineteen-acre lake and campground tucked in the trees.

State Highway 21, which bisects part of the Sabine, follows the historic El Camino Real, the King's Highway. Early Spanish missionaries followed the road to East Texas outposts in their quest to convert Indians to Christianity. Later, this part of Texas became a no man's land. Murderers and thieves lurked in the woods alongside El Camino Real, preying on travelers and fanning the West's reputation as a land of outlaws.

Like early adventurers, contemporary explorers often choose to see the forest on horseback or on foot, particularly Indian Mound Wilderness. Primarily a pine forest, the wilderness also has zones where hardwoods such as oaks and beeches grow. The wilderness is named for mounds once thought to have been built by Indians, but now attributed to sudden bouts of erosion followed by rapid regrowth of vegetation. Many wildflowers are found in the area. The colorful

Carolina Lily, a large orange-red blossom with purplish brown spots and a yellow throat, abounds in the area.

Throughout the Texas forests, managers are striving to protect areas where sensitive plants grow, as well as places with particular scenic value. Two spots receiving special attention in the Sabine are Beech Ravines and Colorow Creek, both in the middle of the forest near San Augustine. The yellow dogtooth violet grows in both locations, along with two other plants rare in Texas. Beech Ravines, along the steep shorelines of Toledo Bend Reservoir, features deep ditches formed by erosion harboring lush growths of ferns and flowering plants.

Further west, Colorow Creek has excavated a twelve-foot-deep ravine through sandstone, leaving a rock bridge over the narrow divide. The shaded slopes support a profusion of spring wildflowers. There are also rock outcrops, a small waterfall, and a miniature box canyon.

Like the Sabine, the Angelina National Forest attracts many of its visitors because of a large lake, in this case the Sam Rayburn Reservoir. The Angelina, 154,245 acres, is predominantly a pine forest of shortleaf, longleaf, and loblolly varieties. The forest is named for a Hanina Indian woman mentioned in the writings of early French and Spanish explorers. Although few details about her are known,

White-tailed deer, squirrel, and dove are popular game animals in Texas national forests. PHOTO COURTESY OF USDA FOREST SERVICE - OLIVER D. BOUNDS

her name is also affixed to a river and a county, the only Texas county named for a woman.

There are seven campgrounds in the Angelina. Most are located on two sides of the Rayburn Reservoir, but Boykin Springs is farther west near a spring-fed lake stocked with rainbow trout during the winter. A massive stone fireplace warms the picnic shelter built by the Civilian Conservation Corps at Boykin Springs in the 1930s. The Sawmill Hiking Trail begins at the campground and travels for 5.5 miles along the Neches River to another campground at Bouton Lake. An abandoned railroad spur leads to remnants of an early sawmill.

Longleaf pines dominate in the sandy soils in this part of the forest and are managed through prescribed burnings that replicate the wildfires once common to this region. Seeps which occur in the area are the focus of great botanical interest. These are damp places where sandy soils lie atop impermeable sandstone. Amazing varieties of plants thrive in seeps. Sphagnum moss, three fern species, two kinds of insect-trapping sundews, pitcher plants, bog buttons, bog violets, and rose pogonia orchids are only some of them. The yellow fringeless orchid, rare in Texas, and bog coneflower, under consideration as endangered, are also found here. A few wide-open prairies, called barrens, also exist in the Angelina. The endangered Navasota ladies' tresses, a cream-colored orchid, grows on the fringes of one of these barrens. More flowering plants, dense pine forests, and clear water streams are in the Angelina's two wilderness areas, Upland Island and Turkey Hill.

Above: *Wild turkeys have been reintroduced in parts of the forests.* BILL LEA
Right: *The Angelina River is named for an Indian woman.* ROBERT W. PARVIN

Davy Crockett · Sam Houston

The Big Slough Canoe Trail follows an often slow-moving loop of water down the Neches River and through the Big Slough Wilderness. Water levels are often sufficient for the trip, especially in winter and spring. Fallen trees, however, sometimes bar the way. Then floaters must carry their crafts around the obstructions, just like Indians and pioneers once were forced to do.

The canoe trail is part of the Davy Crockett National Forest, named for the fighter for Texas independence who died at the battle of the Alamo. The loss of Crockett and his fellow soldiers spurred on others who ultimately succeeded in winning separation from Mexico. For a time, Texas was an independent nation with a single star on its flag. Located west of Lufkin, the 161,497-acre forest includes one major recreation area at Ratcliff Lake. A campground with an amphitheater for summer programs and a forty-five-acre lake for swimming, fishing, and boating are some of the attractions. Paddle boats and canoes are available to rent at a small concession stand. Only electric motors are allowed in the lake, which is stocked with bass, bream, and catfish.

The high-pitched whir of saws once reverberated across Ratcliff Lake, used as a log holding pond by the Central Coal and Coke Company Sawmill, which operated until 1920. The 4-C National Recreation Trail, named for the lumber company, is twenty miles long and starts at the campground. Restricted to hikers, the trail cuts across boggy lowlands and upland pine forests, plunges through the Big Slough Wilderness, then finishes dramatically at Neches Bluff. The bluff stands about 100 feet above the

Spider lilies thrive in the marshes of the Davy Crockett National Forest, named for the frontiersman who died at the Alamo.
LAURENCE PARENT

RESTORATION

Some 1,600 acres in the Sam Houston National Forest reflect the spirit of cooperation that can lead to restoration of abused land. The area was clearcut and stripped of topsoil by an oil company. With donations of treated sludge from the City of Houston, Ranger Joe Carmical and other Forest Service workers began to heal the eroded surface. Then Quail Unlimited donated $10,000 to grow millet, sunflowers, and other plants attractive to wildlife, including neotropical birds such as white-eyed vireos, painted buntings, and warblers that spend winters in South and Central America.

Donations of time came from Exxon Company USA employees, who built eighty nesting boxes for bluebirds, wood ducks, and screech owls; from the Boy Scouts, who also built bird houses; and from the Telephone Pioneers of America, who donated and installed poles for the bird boxes. Turkey, quail, and deer are being released into the area, which is fast becoming an active wildlife habitat where once there was devastation.

Left: *A vivid painted bunting.*
JOHN SNYDER
Above: *Forest Service employee Dawn Carrie captures a yellow-breasted chat.* PHOTO COURTESY OF USDA FOREST SERVICE - OLIVER D. BOUNDS

Neches River, with a commanding view of the forest. Piney Creek Horse Trail covers fifty-two miles of ground farther south and west and has an equestrian camp with a trailhead off Forest Road 525.

The Sam Houston Forest of 161,154 acres is less than an hour's drive from the outskirts of bustling Houston, the nation's fourth-largest city. An interrupted arc of patches of government land separated by private property, the forest is named for the commander-in-chief of the forces for Texas independence. After their victory, Texans elected Houston their first president of the new nation of Texas.

The forest is stitched together by the Lone Star Trail, 140 miles long. Maintained by Sierra Club volunteers, the trail starts at one end near the town of Cleveland, then moves north and west. Hikers soon cross Winters Bayou where there is a clear stream, normally fifty feet wide or more, that spills in a series of shallow rapids and forms quiet pools. Dogwoods, fragrant wax myrtle, and palmettos knit tightly together nearby.

For the first twenty-seven miles, the foot path is a

national recreation trail. One of the highlights along this stretch is Big Creek Scenic Area. Four loop trails, all less than a mile, course through the section noted for plant diversity and stately trees. Viewing wildlife is always a likely possibility. Bluebirds, warblers, screech owls, and other birds inhabit the woods. Deer sightings are also frequent. Hunting, popular throughout most of the Texas national forests, is prohibited here, along with camping.

The trail continues to Double Lake Recreation Area, one of two major forest campgrounds, both built in the 1930s by the Civilian Conservation Corps. Swimming, boating, and fishing are popular in the forty-two acre lake and rental boats are available.

Past a primitive camp farther on for hikers, the Lone Star Trail leaves the national forest and threads along roadways through big patches of private land interspersed with more national forest. After some sixty miles, the trail reaches the last part of the forest, which surrounds Lake Conroe's northern shores. Popular among Houstonians for water skiing, sailing, and houseboating, the 21,000-acre lake is also renowned among anglers for black bass.

Near Stubblefield Recreation Area, the other principal campground, endangered red-cockaded woodpeckers are the focus of recovery efforts in a nearby demonstration site. Forty trees with nest cavities stand on about seventy acres located beside Forest Road 215. Hardwoods are being eliminated in spots and artificial nesting cavities are inserted in pines to assist the birds.

The Lone Star Trail passes through Stubblefield Campground, nestled on the waters of a narrow finger of Lake Conroe. Nearby are trails for off-road vehicles where dirt bikers enjoy careening around curves. The Little Lake Creek Wilderness is near the lake, and the Lone Star Trail also winds through it. In places once dominated by pines, hardwoods such as oak and hickory now thrive. In the 1980s, pine beetles killed many pines and more were cut to stem the infestation. This opened the way for the hardwoods to grow, just part of the ever-changing forest. ♣

The rising sun is easily spotted in the big sky country of the Davy Crockett National Forest. LAURENCE PARENT

Caddo • Lyndon B. Johnson
NATIONAL GRASSLANDS DIRECTORY

POINTS OF INTEREST

Coffee Mill Lake The largest body of water in the Caddo Grassland, covering 750 acres. From Paris, take U. S. Hwy. 82 to Honey Grove, then go north on Farm-to-Market Road 100 into the Caddo Grassland. The lake is located adjacent to Forest Service Road 919.

Ball Knob Hill Among the highest points in north central Texas with a wide-ranging view. From Dallas or Fort Worth, take Interstate 35 to Denton. Go west on U. S. Hwy. 380 to Decatur. Turn west on U. S. Hwy. 81/287 to the town of Alvord. Go east on Ball Knob Road.

RECREATIONAL OPPORTUNITIES

Hiking and Riding No developed trails, but ample open country for both activities. Some fences restrict access.

Camping No developed campsites, but dispersed camping is allowed. Camping is also permitted in picnic areas near the lakes.

Hunting Quail, dove, squirrel, rabbits, and deer. Deer hunting pressure is heavy in the LBJ Grassland and the success rate is low. State license required and state regulations apply. Parts of the Caddo are in a Wildlife Management Area with special regulations.

Fishing Bass, bream, and catfish stocked in the lakes. State license required and state regulations apply.

Off-Road Vehicles About 500 acres of the Caddo have been set aside for off-road use. Check with ranger station for locations.

ADMINISTRATIVE OFFICES

Forest Headquarters 701 N. First Street, Lufkin, TX 75901 (409) 639-8501

National Grasslands FM Road 730 South, P. O. Box 507, Decatur, TX 76234 (817) 627-5475

Sabine • Angelina
NATIONAL FORESTS DIRECTORY

POINTS OF INTEREST

Red Hills Lake Recreation Area Scenic campground adjacent to a small lake in the Sabine National Forest. Take State Hwy. 87 north from Hemphill, for 10.5 miles.

Mill Creek Cove Old-growth American beech and Southern magnolia trees stand in a protected cove in the Sabine. From Hemphill, take State Hwy. 83 east towards Toledo Bend Reservoir. The area is about a mile north and east of Harpers Chapel Church. A trail is planned to the cove.

Upper Colorow Creek Scenic area with many wildflowers and a small rock bridge in the Sabine. From San Augustine, go east on State Hwy. 21. Turn north on Farm-to-Market Road 330. Turn west on Forest Service Road

198. Hike north from the Cordrey Cemetery. A hiking trail is planned for the area.

Boykin Springs Pleasant camping in a scenic area of the Angelina National Forest. Take U.S. Hwy. 69 east from Lufkin to Zavalla. Take State Hwy. 63 east for eleven miles. Turn south on Forest Service Road 313.

WILDERNESS

Indian Mounds 11,037 acres adjacent to Toledo Bend Reservoir in the Sabine. Named for the peculiar "potato hills," the wilderness is near the Indian Mounds Campground.

Upland Island 12,650 acres in the southern portion of the Angelina. Areas along Graham Creek and the Neches River are boggy and feature cypress trees.

Turkey Hill 5,286 acres in the northeast of the Angelina Forest. Like the Indian Mounds and the Upland Island, it is crisscrossed with primitive trails.

RECREATIONAL OPPORTUNITIES

Hiking and Riding Short trails are found near most major campgrounds. Wildernesses offer opportunities for both horseback riders and hikers.

Camping Both developed facilities and primitive sites in both forests. Dispersed camping is allowed in most parts of both forests except during deer hunting season in November and December.

Hunting Deer, squirrel, quail, dove, and duck. State license required and state regulations apply. Wildlife management areas are used to improve game populations.

Fishing Small lakes are stocked with trout. Streams support warmwater fish. Most fishing is for bass in the large reservoirs.

ADMINISTRATIVE OFFICES

Forest Headquarters 701 N. First Street, Lufkin, TX 75901 (409) 639-8501

Sabine Forest:
Tenaha Ranger District 101 South Bolivar, San Augustine, TX 75972 (409) 275-2632

Yellowpine Ranger District 201 South Palm, P. O. Box F, Hemphill, TX 75948 (409) 787-3870

Angelina Forest:
Angelina Ranger District 1907 Atkinson Drive, P. O. Box 756, Lufkin, TX 75901 (409) 639-8620

Davy Crockett • Sam Houston
NATIONAL FORESTS DIRECTORY

POINTS OF INTEREST

Ratcliff Lake Recreation Area In the Davy Crockett National Forest. Camping, swimming, fishing, and other activities. A trailhead is located near the campground for the 4-C hiking trail. Take Interstate 45 between Houston and Dallas. Go on State Hwy. 7 east through Crockett, Texas, and into the national forest.

Big Creek Scenic Area 1,420 acres in the Sam Houston National Forest set aside for viewing pleasure. No hunting or camping allowed. Take U.S. Hwy. 59 north from Houston through Cleveland to the town of Shepherd. Go west on Farm-to-Market Road 2666 into the national forest. Turn right onto Forest Service Road 217.

Stubblefield Lake Recreation Area In the Sam Houston forest adjacent to Lake Conroe and the Lone Star Trail. Take Interstate 45 north from Houston to New Waverly. Go west for eleven miles on Farm-to-Market Road 1375. Turn right on Forest Service Road 215 for three miles.

WILDERNESS

Big Slough 3,639 acres of primarily hardwood forest in the Davy Crockett Forest. The 4-C hiking trail passes through the wilderness.

Little Lake Creek 4,000 acres of pine and hardwood forest. Some dirt embankments once served as beds for logging railroads. The Lone Star Trail passes through the area.

RECREATIONAL OPPORTUNITIES

Hiking and Riding The Lone Star National Recreation Trail travels 140 miles through the Sam Houston Forest and the 4-C National Recreation Trail explores twenty miles of the Crockett. There are fifty-two miles of horseback riding trails in the Crockett south of Ratcliff Lake. There is also horseback riding permitted in the Sam Houston forest.

Camping Dispersed camping is allowed in most areas of the forests except during deer hunting season in November and December. Hunters use primitive hunt camps.

Hunting Deer, squirrel, quail, dove, and waterfowl. Wild turkeys are being reintroduced. State license required and state regulations apply.

Fishing Both Lake Conroe and Lake Livingston, which is just east of the Sam Houston Forest, are known for year-round fishing for black bass. Catfish, bream, and bass are stocked in Lake Ratcliff.

Canoeing Big Slough Canoe Trail in the Crockett offers a true wilderness experience. Lakes by major campgrounds are also popular spots for canoeing.

Off-Road Vehicles Open-country and trails set aside for these vehicles in the Sam Houston Forest.

ADMINISTRATIVE OFFICES

Forest Headquarters 701 N. First Street, Lufkin, TX 75901 (409) 639-8501

Davy Crockett:
Neches Ranger District East Loop 304, Crockett, TX 75835 (409) 544-2046

Trinity Ranger District P. O. Box 130, Apple Springs, TX 75926 (409) 831-2246

Sam Houston:
San Jacinto Ranger District 308 North Belcher, Cleveland, TX 77327 (713) 592-6462

Raven Ranger District FM 1375 P. O. Drawer 1000, New Waverly, TX 77358 (409) 344-6205

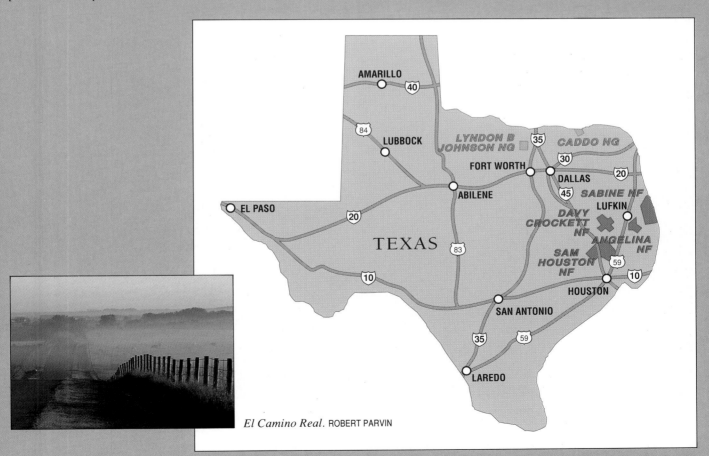

El Camino Real. ROBERT PARVIN

Everyone from paupers to kings can enjoy incomparable sunrises for free within the national forests of the South, including the start of a day along the Cumberland River in Kentucky's Daniel Boone National Forest. Protecting the forests' air, soil, water, vegetation, and wildlife are juggled with competing interests. ADAM JONES

Conclusion

Striving for balance

Visitors to the national forests of the South return home with lasting impressions of incomparable beauty. Hillsides dressed in the purple-pink blooms of rhododendrons. Primeval black-water swamps, dense with aged cypress, where the eerie call of a barred owl echoes through the stillness. Sunsets viewed from mountaintops, the evening sky dissolving into a whorl of color.

For hikers, anglers, picnicking families, and countless others who see and appreciate their splendor, our national forests are like precious jewels to be treasured and protected. And the value of these lands will only escalate in the future, as a growing population, hungry for an unspoiled place in nature, finds its way into the national forests of the South.

With increasing numbers of visitors come both mounting pressures to accommodate their interests, and potential conflicts with traditional forest activities. Campers and hikers may find logging unsightly and disruptive of the tranquil outdoor experience they seek. Loggers, for their part, already resent increasing restrictions on the amount of timber available for harvest. As vast as they are, our national forests may not be vast enough to satisfy the interests of everyone. Choices will have to be made, and many of these decisions will not be easy.

Further complicating the equation are considerations for living things that cannot speak for themselves. National forests are often the last refuge for plants and animals whose habitats beyond forest boundaries are rapidly disappearing. In Southern forests alone are seventy-seven of the plants and animals found on the federal list of endangered species. "Endangered" means they are at risk of extinction. Another thirty-six species are considered "threatened," and nineteen more may soon join their ranks. Added to these are more than 800 other species considered "sensitive," in need of close observation to detect any declines in their populations or well-being.

The Forest Service is not standing idly by while these creatures struggle for survival. Wildlife specialists, often in cooperation with experts from other agencies, are protecting habitats and, in some cases, reintroducing species. In Kentucky, thirty osprey have been successfully released in the Daniel Boone National Forest during a four-year program. Biologists patiently nurtured the fledglings for weeks before they were old enough to fly. As a result, boaters on Kentucky waters in the Daniel Boone may once again watch this magnificent bird fall from the sky and plunge into the water to snare a fish. In Arkansas, endangered bats are shielded from human harassment within their cave retreats after the Forest Service erected gates across cave openings, allowing free access to the bats, but keeping visitors at a safe distance.

Protecting various species, enhancing recreation for a clamoring public—these are only two of the immense challenges facing caretakers of the forests.

They must also see that the woodlands fulfill their founding purposes of protecting precious watersheds while providing timber and other consumable resources.

Conflicts among proponents for these various interests are sometimes inevitable. Whenever possible, compromise is sought. Traditionally open to hunting, national forests now also accommodate those who want to watch wildlife in areas where hunting is prohibited. Increased sensitivity to the visual effects of logging has fostered creation of special scenic areas, where trees are cut with particular care not to mar the beauty of the landscape.

These and other compromises are affected through the direct involvement of both private individuals and groups. National forests, like major corporations, are managed according to detailed, long-range plans, with recommendations from experts in many fields. The public, as owner of the forests, also has a say in how they should be managed. As years pass and considerations change, the plans are updated and revised, and public comment and ideas are invited. In fact, Forest Service plans are always open for inspection, and forest supervisors welcome your interest.

And there are other ways to take part. As tax dollars grow scarce, the importance of volunteer involvement grows. Every forest can benefit from donated labor. Many forest managers have tasks waiting to be done, but no one to call upon. Age, education, and physical ability are no limits. Young children and senior citizens alike are daily performing duties that benefit all forest visitors.

Left: Different from national parks, national forests serve as resources for various needs, including timber. BILL LEA
Above right: *Osprey have been successfully reintroduced on the Daniel Boone National Forest.* BILL LEA
Below right: *Hungry for the unspoiled outdoors, campers and other nature enthusiasts are increasingly drawn to national forests. This idyllic scene is found at Cliffside lake campground in the Nantahala National Forest.* BILL LEA

Individuals can play crucial roles in preserving the beauty of our national forests. Carelessness and arson continue to be the principal causes of wildfire, which every year blackens thousands of acres and needlessly risks the lives of firefighters. Thoughtless people foul the landscape with trash and graffiti. Forest Service employees, including the highest ranking supervisors, routinely pick up litter as they move through the woodlands—a habit all of us could emulate.

In an age of dwindling open spaces, our national forests beckon, offering a respite from the crush of crowds. Within some Southern forests it is still possible to travel for many miles and never encounter another soul. Walking along narrow trails, passing clear flowing streams: here is a glimpse of the untamed land that once existed throughout the country. The only sounds are those of the residents, the songbirds flitting through the trees, a squirrel rummaging through the old leaves on the ground. Visit the national forests, and share their quiet corners and secret gardens. You will want to return again and again. ♣